the life and music of

MARK HEARD

HAMMERS & NAILS

the life and music of
MARK HEARD

HAMMERS & NAILS

BY MATTHEW DICKERSON

CORNERSTONE PRESS CHICAGO

CHICAGO ILLINOIS

All song lyrics, except where otherwise noted, are ©Mark Heard and used by permission.

"Life in the Industry: A Musician's Diary" by Mark Heard, first appeared in *Image: A Journal of the Arts and Religion*, 2. (1992).

Published by Cornerstone Press Chicago

939 W. Wilson

Chicago, IL 60640

www.cornerstonepress.com

cspress@jpusa.org

Cover design by Noah Krogh

Book design by Thor Uremovich

Cover photo ©2003 by Joel Russell.

Back cover photo ©2003 by Mark Heard.

Printed in the United States of America

06 05 04 03   5 4 3 2 1

Library of Congress Cataloging-in-Publication Data

Dickerson, Matthew T., 1963-

Hammers & Nails : the life and music of Mark Heard / by Matthew Dickerson.

p. cm.

ISBN 0-940895-49-8 (alk. paper); ISBN 0-940895-50-1 (case bound)

1. Heard, Mark. 2. Singers--United States--Biography. I. Title:

Hammers and Nails. II. Title.

ML420.H337D43 2003

782.42164'092--dc21

2003000792

CONTENTS

[FOREWORD]

Rarely, a singular event or person in our lives stands as brilliant testimony to Something just beyond our grasp. C.S. Lewis called the longing for this Something "sehnsucht" – the unquenchable yearning for More than we can see, the bitter knowledge that we were never made for death and still suffer the dyings of this world daily, the sweetness of small heroics like the nod over coffee between lovers before again taking up the ordinary burdens of daily life.

I met Mark Heard and his sweet wife Janet in 1980. Even then she seemed a life source for him. His booking agent asked me to help find places for this young southern singer/songwriter to perform. After several small tours throughout the rural towns of New England and the occasional limelight performance at the infamous Cambridge coffeehouse, Passim, Mark and I became friends. These tours, and this friendship, were the backbone of what became Fingerprint Records. Mark's songs crystallized many of my own questions, and his great sense of the unbelievably funny and absurd could leave me breathless in laughter.

Mark Heard never fit in well with the pop culture around him. He was a painter, a photographer, a weaver—a builder of things as well as songs—but whatever he did, he kept to the fringes, wary of the center where the culture is ruled by the politics of style and mass-marketing money. He wasn't so much a loner, but he did prefer the less-explored terra: deserts of land and soul that most of us never bother with.

Mark never believed artistic or spiritual growth could be refined down to a system of principles, formulas, timelines, or gimmicks, and he disdained profit margins as a measure of value. Mark wasn't comfortable inside a music industry that oppressed many and benefited few. He had trouble conforming to the safe and oversimplified standard hook-phrases of Christians without Christ and musicians without music. Audiences on the whole did not reward him for walking away from their expectations. He was not a man grooming himself for popular success.

The book you hold in your hand is an abridged collection of conversations recalled by those who connected with Mark on some level, at some point during his brief life. You'll find the road Mark walked, the way he looked at things and the choices he made, were complicated further by the fact that he was a husband and a father. He was someone who wanted more for his wife and daughter than life gives to an artist who chooses to believe the unbelievable truth. His uncompromising standards are what set him not above, but apart from the rest. His untinted reflections on life, no matter how he expressed them, profoundly affect me and many others, even to this day. While his journey may have been stained by his inability to simplify and qualify, he was extremely successful. He stayed true even in the midst of the noise, fog, and delusion. If you believe that Art which awakens you to your own sense of authenticity is vital, rare, and essential, you'll find Mark's music and work addresses a thirst, even while much of what is generated in today's culture seldom does.

This excerpt from his journal is an encouragement to recognize our own souls;

> Maps hide cities, cities hide houses, houses hide faces, faces hide hearts, but hearts still beat quietly. Few feel even their own pulse, but hearts are made to beat. We can drown them out with more accessible rhythms, but they continue the counterpoint. Hearts are made to beat. Our souls are still with us, our creator waits for us to notice as our geographical boundaries are chased around the sun by time, decaying in a fashion some call normal.

This book is full of his lyrics and snapshots which show how his beautiful soul softened hearts, instilled hope, spoke out against injustice, exposed the dark side of gravity's pull, whistled in the wind, and wondered out loud to the stars in the deep desert night.

Mark's love for his wife, and for his little girl, seemed to parallel his approach toward most things. He was passionate, emotional, unsure of himself, angry at his failings, tender to the core. He saw Janet and Rebecca as brilliant and good, and their love was an anchor for his own sense of hope. He ached at the thought of swallowing a lie, turning a blind eye, calculating his steps. As for me, grateful to be his friend, I'll never forget his laugh, his unselfish encouragement, and his undecorated, un-pretty perspectives on the unpopular truth.

Mark believed *Dry Bones Dance, Second Hand,* and *Satellite Sky* were his best recorded works. These titles are all now remastered and rereleased. Any proceeds from the sale of *Hammers And Nails,* the new release, and any proceeds from the sale of his Fingerprint efforts go to Janet and Rebecca. However, what's very important to them—as well as Mark's own intention in making the work—is to convey a hope in the midst of his journey that might inspire each of us to brave believing in our own fingerprint.

PS—Thank you, Holly, for the demo tape in 1979. Thank you, Chuck, for being a true brother to us both. Thank you, Janet, for your sweet, humble heart and shoulder stronger than most. Thank you, Matthew, for collecting these opinions and putting together this glimpse.

—Dan Russell
Fingerprint Records
Newsound International

[PREFACE AND ACKNOWLEDGEMENTS]

Treasure of the broken land

Parched earth give up your captive ones

Waiting wind of Gabriel

Blow soon upon these hollow bones.

Mark Heard penned those lyrics late in the fall of 1991 after spending a week sitting beside a hospital bed watching his father die a grueling death. Less than a year later, while performing at the Cornerstone Festival, Mark fell victim to a heart attack. A second heart attack followed a few days later, leaving Mark in a coma.[1] A month later, Mark went to join his father, and moved—as Bruce Cockburn would later write–"closer to the light."[2]

My personal acquaintance with Mark and his wife Janet began in the summer of 1985, shortly after I had graduated from college. Though I'd seen Mark in concert on several occasions over the previous five years, I'd never met him in person. After attending an all-day outdoor music festival[3] sponsored by New Sound Concerts—a concert where I felt many members of the audience had been rude to Mark during his set—I decided to write a letter to him expressing my appreciation for his music. I had no idea if he would answer such a letter, coming to him out of the blue as it were, and so I was pleasantly surprised when I received a handwritten response from Janet just a few weeks later.

At the time, I didn't pursue any further correspondence. That fall, however, I began graduate school at Cornell University, and I decided to try bringing Mark to campus. The details fell into place, and in the spring of 1986 Mark Heard performed at Cornell University to an audience of about 200. My brief (and ill-fated) foray into concert promotion was quite unprofitable, but it did provide my first real chance to talk with Mark in person, as well as the opportunity to hear him perform again. We corresponded a little more, and the following year—with the help of Logos Bookstore of Ithaca and my friend Scott Adams—I brought Mark to Cornell a second time. Unfortunately, my hope of trying to break even on the concert proved naïve at best, and I couldn't afford to repeat the event a third year. Furthermore, after the commercial letdown of his iDEoLA project, Mark was no longer recording, and was touring less also. We did, however, keep up a sporadic correspondence interspersed with a few phone calls.

In 1989, having completed my degree at Cornell, I moved to Vermont and began teaching at Middlebury College. In the spring of 1990, I helped to bring Mark to the east coast for a concert at Mead Chapel on the Middlebury College campus. By this time, Mark had finally gone back into the studio, and was just in the process of releasing *Dry Bones Dance*. About that same time, my first novel was accepted for publication. Mark had read several of my short stories over the previous two years, and after reading my newly published novel he asked me to help him out with a publishing project of his own. His vision was to organize some of his journal writings, photographs, and unpublished lyrics into a book. He wanted me to help him with both the organization of the material and with finding a publisher. Though I had little experience with that type of writing, the opportunity to see more of Mark's work was exciting, and it was with great eagerness that I agreed to give whatever aid I could. Soon afterward, he sent me some of his material— mostly lyrics for songs that would eventually appear on the album *Satellite Sky*—and we worked for a couple of months on arranging it. Finally we sent it off to the acquisition editors at a few publishing houses.

Unfortunately, the responses we got were all similar. And for those who know much of Mark's history, they were not surprising. An acquisitions editor would read the sample chapter and get excited by the profundity of Mark's writing. The editor and I would have what seemed (to me) like a very positive conversation. He or she would then pass the project on to the marketing department . . . where it would get rejected. However insightful they thought Mark's writing was, the folks in charge of making money didn't see how they could sell the book.

After Mark died in the summer of 1992, I continued to work on the book for another year, but only ran into more dead-ends. Only two things came out of these efforts. In their Spring 1993 issue, *Image Journal* published a short memorial I'd written on Mark.[4] Interested in the quality of art rather than in its commercial value, this newly-formed journal was excited by artists like Mark Heard. In their previous issue—which had been published just around the time of Mark's death—they had printed a collection of his journals titled *Life in the Industry: A Musician's Diary*. This contained some of the material he had planned for the book.

Also in 1993, I was asked by Word Records to write a short biographical sketch for the release of two posthumous Mark Heard projects: *High Noon* and *Strong Hand of Love*. The former was a collection of songs from Mark's final three albums with a pair of unreleased recordings thrown in as a bonus. The latter was a tribute album, with a number of well-known artists covering Mark's songs. At the time I wrote the biographical sketch for Word, Mark's death was still very close to me, both emotionally and chronologically. It affected me as a friend. It affected me as a fellow father, thinking about the wife and young daughter he had left behind. And it affected me as a fan, robbed of one of the world's great songwriters. This sense of recent emotional loss eked out in the sketch.[5]

For several years, this piece I did for Word—more a eulogy than a biographical sketch—was the only public thing that came out of the work I had done, and I'd nearly given up hope on the project ever seeing daylight. Not wanting Mark's work to be lost forever, I began—with the blessing of Fingerprint Records—to make some of his unpublished lyrics available on the Web. But in February of 2001, I received an unexpected e-mail. Chris Rice of Cornerstone Press had seen some of my material on Mark and approached me with the idea of writing a book. When I told him of the project begun years earlier with Mark's photography, journal writings, and unpublished lyrics, Chris's interest grew. I also mentioned that in the years since Mark's death, I'd collected several stories about him from his mother Jean and from Janet, as well as from various friends, agents, and fellow musicians: David and Kate Miner, Pierce Pettis, John Flynn, Holly Benyousky, Dan and Joel Russell, and Brooks Williams. Chris suggested that all the material might be rolled into a single book—part biography and part collection of Mark's own writing—and asked if I would be interested in doing it.

I admit that my initial excitement was mingled with skepticism about whether it would actually get published. It was worth a try, however, if there was a chance it would help bring Mark's work to light for more people. And so, in preparation to write the book, one of the first things I did was to go back and find the piece I had written nearly nine years earlier. As I dug it out of the mothballs of my computer files and reread it, it dawned on me (with some embarrassment) that it was probably just the sort of thing that Mark Heard would have found sappy, preachy and overly simplistic.

There was also at least one error in that sketch. The story of Mark having "turned down a recording contract offer from Columbia Records" in order "to pursue his musical ideologies as an independent" was widely circulated, and at one time included in a biography as part of his promotional press package—a biography which I had used in writing my own sketch. Yet I later discovered from Mark's close friend Tim Alderson that this story was incomplete and misleading. As Tim tells:

> The fact is, that contract was offered in the days when twenty-one was the legal age for entering into a contract. As such, the contract needed his father's signature. Despite all Mark's pleadings to the contrary, his father refused to sign the contract believing it was not in Mark's best interest to pursue a career in music at that time. He wanted Mark to finish college and build the foundation for a real job.
>
> Through all Mark's struggles in the christian music business and particularly when he felt most trapped, he would think back to his dad's refusal to sign that contract and lament what might have been. He felt like he had missed the only opportunity he would ever have to pursue a meaningful career in music.

This knowledge certainly put a different spin on the next sentence in my sketch: "This decision would characterize him for many years to come."

Nonetheless, despite the aforementioned faults of this sketch, the words were basically true, and as I reread them there was a resurfacing of all the emotions I'd felt when Mark first died: loss, frustration, anger, grief, and confusion. And I knew I was not alone in those feelings. Every person I had talked with over the intervening years—especially those who had been closest to Mark and had known best his many human faults and weaknesses—had wrestled with the same emotions. Indeed, if anything can be said about how my own thoughts have changed since that time, it is that I've come to appreciate Mark Heard's music even more since his death.

Now that I have spent many hours with several of his close friends and family members I have come to learn more about Mark Heard as a person. If there was one other major flaw with my earlier piece, it was probably that I had given in to the temptation to try to make Mark a martyr: the Brilliant-Unrecognized-Poet-Mistreated-by-the-Industry view of his life. As Mark's close friend Pat Terry pointed out, "This whole image of Mark as some kind of martyred genius, he would have hated that because, quite frankly, he just lived and worked." Pat went on to explain:

Any time you write things that people appreciate, it becomes a part of their lives, and it becomes an inspiration in their lives. Mark has been that for a lot of people. What people need to understand was that for Mark it was just work that he did his best to be honest about. He never felt like he was sharing great jewels of wisdom for anyone to live their lives by or anything. He would have been embarrassed at that concept.

Along those lines, in an interview in 1987, Mark commented: "I hate to use the term artist because I'm just a guy who makes noise." Mark found it difficult even to discuss the song-writing process. He didn't seem even to have a "process": "I don't know how to talk about writing songs, which I know is annoying for anybody trying to find out my thoughts on those things, but it's really something that's not a totally conscious process. Writing's not something I can sit down and quantify."[6]

There was one exception: a brief period in the '80s when, as Pat described:

> [Mark] wrote some things in an attempt to be mainstream. They were quite good, but they were different from his other things. You could hear that they were more crafted songs—well-crafted, but they did not have the Reality down inside of him that his other songs had. He grew frustrated with that very quickly. He just said, "That's not what I do."

In any case, there were many factors contributing to the lack of commercial success that Mark Heard received in his lifetime. Certainly the commercial nature of the industry did play a role: neither artistic integrity, nor honesty, nor even musical talent are necessarily the ingredients that make something (or someone) marketable. But one also has to take into account Mark's own stubbornness. As his friends Chuck Long and Pat Terry pointed out in their interview with me, Mark did indeed pursue commercial success. He was not ambivalent toward it, but rather had a strong desire for his music to be accepted into mainstream pop culture. But time after time, he would say or do things that would directly interfere with this goal. In Mark's own words:

> Anybody who [makes music] in a social context has the frustration of having to make a living doing it, and that revolves around having companies distribute your work, and pressures that dictate how far you might be able to go, or which directions you may want to lean with the way your music is structured. But that's

a struggle anybody who does this has to live with. Some people live with it very easily and throw away their self-identities in favor of doing something they know the public will buy, or hope the public will buy. I certainly hope people will buy my record, but I don't live in order to do what people want . . . [7]

Then, too, there was simply the aspect of luck: being in the right place at the right time. Ten years after Mark's death, there has been a major resurgence of the singer-songwriter tradition and the whole corresponding Americana culture, with several commercially successful artists (such as Gillian Welch) riding a wave that did not exist a decade and a half earlier when Mark was recording. Add to that the incredible explosion of the Internet, with its much-expanded opportunity for independent labels and artists to get their names (and products) out, and you have conditions today under which Mark Heard may well have been very successful commercially—were he still alive and recording. In short, though there are some important grains of truth to the ideas behind the Misunderstood Martyr understanding of Mark Heard's life, it is by no means the complete picture, nor is it the purpose of this book to portray him in such a light.

In any case, I continued to correspond with Chris Rice, and put together a few sample chapters. And over the next few months—with the help of Janet Heard, Dan Russell, and Holly Benyousky—I got in touch with several more people who had known Mark well. Slowly the book came together. Not all the interviews were easy. Almost a decade had passed since Mark's death. While some memories of Mark had grown even sharper, some had faded. And whether sharp or not, many were painful. But nearly everybody I met was eager to help. The stories I heard were witty, profound, comic, and at times, tragic. They were also far too many to share in one book. I hope the stories I have chosen will help paint a clearer picture of who Mark was for those who never had the privilege of knowing him—not a simpler picture, because Mark was a complex person, but at least a clearer picture of those complexities.

Perhaps of greater interest to the many Mark Heard fans around the world, this book also contains what has proven to be a treasure to me: a collection of Mark's lyrics that were never published or recorded, as well as a small handful of excerpts from previously unpublished journals and letters. This book also provided the necessary impetus for a companion CD of previously unreleased Mark Heard songs taken from various demo recordings made during the final few years of his life.

With respect to the "biography" (for lack of a better word), I have chosen not to present Mark's life in a strictly chronological fashion. In fact, it is not so much a biography but a collection of snapshots, vignettes, and memories of Mark that give some insight into who he was and what it was that he accomplished. If you are bothered by the backward (and forward) jumps, I can only defend my choice by the following: (1) the simple approach didn't seem to do justice to the complex person, (2) there were thematic arrangements that seemed to fit better than chronological ones. And if neither of those work for you, then (3) I was following some vague aesthetic authorial sense.

As I conclude my preface, I make one final comment, which summarizes some of my own concerns and the concerns of many of Mark's closest friends regarding my writing of this book. *Hammers and Nails* is—both by design and by necessity—a mosaic and not a photograph. In a letter to me, written shortly before this book went to print but after he had read a draft of it, Tim Alderson compared what I had done to the cover of Mark's album *Mosaics,* (the design and concept which came from Tim):

> I had a photograph of Mark's face printed on a 12-inch square piece of paper and then cut that print into 144 1-inch squares. Each square was numbered and then sent along with a corresponding 2-inch square of blank paper to one of Mark's many friends around the world with the instruction to render on the blank paper exactly what was seen on the photo fragment using any medium that suited their fancy. Some portions of the photo, of course, were simply black. In these cases folks were given the freedom to do as they pleased with their white paper. The plan was to get back all the 2-inch squares and reassemble the photo from these pieces.
>
> The plan obviously worked visually, but it worked on so many deeper levels. It was a truly moving experience for Mark to have all these people participate in this way. It also made for a pretty entertaining album cover credit.
>
> The point of recounting this story is to illustrate the true value of the stories in your book. Taken alone or even in groups, they, like the pieces of the portrait on the *Mosaics* cover, don't communicate much of anything. However, when placed in a much larger context, they can start to fill in the blanks.

And, much like that album cover, the portrait painted in your book is clearly an image of Mark, but it is also clearly an imperfect one. Looking closely at the album cover will reveal another similarity with your book which is that some of the pieces missed the mark altogether and yet still somehow, taken all together, these pieces give us an image that tells us something about Mark and a lot about those who knew and admired him.

The last paragraph was a little humbling to me, but I include it because I think Tim's point needs to be made. If you really want to understand Mark's music, then listen to it. If you skip all the stories I've collected about Mark in this book, and ignore everything I've written, you can still learn quite a bit by reading the collection of Mark's lyrics and journals contained in this project.

Thanks to the many people who spent time sharing stories and memories to make this project possible: Tim Alderson, John Austin, Holly Benyousky, Chris Christian, John Flynn, Jason Harrod, Chris Hauser, Janet Heard, Jean Heard, Susan Heard, Steve Hindalong, Tom Howard, Chuck Long, Bill Mallonee, Phil Madeira, Buddy Miller, Steve (Tonio) K., David Miner, Kate Miner, Pierce Pettis, Dan Russell, Joel Russell, Randy Stonehill, Pat Terry, Tom Willett, and Brooks Williams. I also offer my apologies to all of you out there who had many more stories to tell, and whom I never got the chance to talk with.

Thanks to Holly Benyousky, Janet Heard, Dan Russell, and Martin Stillion for helping set up various interviews, and to Denise Heath for help in transcribing them. Dan also needs to be acknowledged for many conversations about Mark over the past ten years that were never recorded (and thus are not cited in the book) and yet which form a background texture over which many of the other (more formal) interviews are painted. Thanks to Pat Terry and Janet for reading several drafts along the way, and for their helpful and insightful feedback. Thanks also to Steve Bertolino for proofreading the first couple chapters for the pre-release booklet distributed at Cornerstone in Summer 2002.

Most especially, thanks to Jean Heard and Janet Heard for sharing Mark with us all, and to Rebecca Heard for letting us use some family photographs.

—Matthew Dickerson, 2002

[EXPLANATION OF GENERAL FORMAT]

On footnoting: Much of the material in the book came from, or was based upon, interviews of family, friends, and acquaintances of Mark Heard. The interviewees are listed at the end of the text. Where applicable, I have also included the dates and locations of the interviews. Interviews that took place via electronic mail (correspondence) are noted as such. Some interviews—mostly notably with Janet Heard—spanned several months both before and during the writing of this book, and included conversations in-person, over-the-phone, and via e-mail. In order to avoid the distraction of countless footnotes (due to the large amount of interview material used in this book) I have chosen not to footnote each quote. In particular, where the source of cited material or opinion is clear from context, the reader is referred to the list of interviews at the end. Footnotes are included only in such places where either the source is not evident from context, or where I have used material from sources other than interviews.

On capitalization: For reasons that may become clear from reading this book, where the term christian is used as an adjective to refer to an inanimate object or entity—such as in "christian music" or "christian business"—I have left the term uncapitalized. When the word "Christian" refers to a person or belief, however, I use the more common convention of capitalizing the first letter. (The exception is when I am quoting from a written work, in which case I quote directly keeping the convention used by the quoted source.)

[Mark Heard, Saguaro National Park, AZ, 1992.]

{1}

I JUST WANNA GET WARM

"Mark Heard was one of the

single funniest people I ever met,

and one of the most sincere."

–Pierce Pettis

BIG WHEELS ROLL

1992, *Satellite Sky*

Twenty years on and he still thinks
He'll make a dent on the shrinking world
But the pent-up way it works still stinks
The spinning of wheels has been enough
To keep him occupied, keep him tough
But there's no momentum, just the gravel and the spinning.
Those who could help him disappear
Saying "wish we could, but we'd interfere"
After all, they have their own careers

Look up, look down, look out somehow
Look through the blindfold
Shake your fist and bet your soul
You're in the way and the big wheels roll

No one gets on a leaky ship
"Associations weaken one's place
In history" he tells himself
He tells himself they're lame and weak
But he only has himself to blame
For being scatterbrained and quarantined
How can one fool one's self so long?
How can one hold the dream so tight
He chokes it and provokes a wrong?

Look up, look down, look out somehow
Look through the blindfold
Shake your fist and bet your soul

You're in the way and the big wheels roll

He says, "Damn the cool-headed and the setters of goals
Who can feel no evil, no heat, no cold
And who wouldn't know passion if it swallowed them whole.
To whom true love is a left-brain risk
For whom the giving of life is a needless myth
Who cover their graves with monoliths
Cool heads prevail, and we'll become extinct
Mutants too unfit to wish"
That's the fallout of our fingerprints.

Look up, look down, look out somehow
Look through the blindfold
Shake your fist and bet your soul
You're in the way and the big wheels roll

BEFORE I COULD FASHION MY POVERTY

John Mark Heard III was born in Macon, Georgia at 8:45 a.m. on December 16, 1951, the son of John Mark Heard Jr. and Jean Chase Parkins Heard. Jean was twenty-five years old when she gave birth on a Sunday morning. Her husband had just turned thirty.

Some fifty years later, Jean Heard's memories of that time are still fresh. As she recalls, her son's love of music started very early in his life. While Mark was still *in utero*, Jean attended a string concert at Wesleyan College. The room was small and she was sitting in the front row, close to the musicians. There was one particular piece, Fritz Kreisler's "Liebesfreud," which drew an interesting response from her soon-to-be-born son. "The violinist played [that song]," she relates, "and I felt the baby turning over and over [in the womb]." After the performance, she purchased a recording of the piece to bring home. "I played it standing in front of the record player, and the [baby's] turning began again." Convinced that the child within her had taken a liking to "Liebesfreud" and was responding within the womb, Jean played the song over and over again during the last few weeks of her pregnancy. "He liked it after he was born, too!" she concludes.

Mark never took up violin, but when he was three-and-a-half years old he began picking out songs on his little toy piano. The first tune he learned was the theme of *Captain Kangaroo*. Impressed with his abilities, the Heard family bought a real piano the next year: a birthday present for Jean, it was called, but Jean and everybody else knew it was really for Mark. Soon after that, Mark started taking lessons with Herb and Mary Archer, a couple in the music program of the Heards' church.

Like his love of music, Mark's interest in nature also started early. The Heard family lived on a street with lots of pets and children. One morning when Mark was four years old, he looked out his living room window to see two dogs mating on the front lawn. Mark was confused by the strange display, and asked his mother what they were doing. Embarrassed, Jean ended up having to explain to Mark the facts of life—or at least the facts of a dog's life: that this was the way the Lord had made it possible for dogs to have puppies. Mark smiled and shook his head. "How in the world did He ever think of that?!"

When Mark grew older, he also took up an interest in butterflies and moths. He gathered quite a collection, which he mounted in a box acquired from the nearby museum of arts and sciences. He soon joined a lepidopterist society, and during his teen years began corresponding with a professor at Georgia Tech who sold him eggs to hatch. Eventually, he entered his collection of moths in a fair and won a prize for the "Best Butterfly Collection." He accepted the prize, but left the fair disgusted that the judge didn't know the difference between a butterfly and a moth.

One Christmas morning, Jean received a cross-stitch of butterflies from her son. Mark had photographed each butterfly (nine altogether) and designed the cross-stitch pattern himself. Jean was astounded at the beauty of the gift, but even more so at his labor of love when she learned he had spent nine months working on it. "This is for all the times you stopped by the roadside and let me take pictures or collect butterflies," his note said.

Mark's sister Susan put this gift in the context of a broader reflection on how important Mark's artistic and creative side was to his whole personality:

> He had a talent for so many things . . . music, art, photography. He would have an interest and figure out how to incorporate it into an art form. He built a lot of the furniture that Janet and Rebecca still use. He decided one Christmas to knit our Daddy a scarf and hat and got Janet to teach him how to knit so he could make this especially for Daddy. He also had Janet teach him how to needlepoint, and made my parents a beautiful framed piece with different butterflies, to represent all the times they had pulled the car over by the side of the road to let him get out to get a specimen of a certain kind of butterfly (he studied these very intently for several years). He was very interested in the American Indian, and was working on a Navajo rug before he died. He got a Navajo lady to teach him how to weave and then built a loom on which to make his. He never finished it.

WHY, MAMA, WHY?

Mark's love of beauty stayed with him for the rest of his life, as did his sense of humor, and his keen observer's eye. The three were interwoven in him. Unfortunately, during his adult life, the necessity of paying the rent and buying groceries often interfered with his aesthetic pursuits. In order to support himself financially, and also to have the freedom to make his own records, Mark had to take a lot of additional work not related to his own songwriting and recording. It was often said that he burned the candle at both ends.

Among the odd jobs he took on in order to make ends meet, Mark played occasional gigs at local clubs and bars. The expectation in such a scene is that the band will play lots of familiar cover tunes. And anybody who has ever performed cover tunes as background music in a noisy bar knows it's not always a lot of fun, nor is it particularly challenging or interesting for songwriters and musicians of Mark's caliber. Nonetheless, Mark seemed to find something to appreciate in the situation. "Most people think that bar owners only use music as a come-on in order to sell drinks," he wrote in his journals, "[But I] met a lot of owners of bars and clubs that I really respected—there were so many lovely individual stories. One couple's lifelong dream had been to open a bar where there could be music they liked and people to hear it."

On one particular night, Mark's friend David Miner was playing bass at the regular Tuesday night gig David and Kate Miner had at The 8121: the downstairs room of the infamous Coconut Teaszer in Los Angeles. Mark was filling in for Kate, who for some reason or other couldn't perform her usual spot that night. As David tells the story, Mark was in a lively mood, throwing cigars to the audience every time he finished a song. During a pause when they were asking for audience requests, David dared Mark to sing in its entirety Chuck Berry's "Maybelline"—about the wordiest song anybody would ever have thought of—*while smoking a cigar.*

Mark didn't just take the challenge; he loved it. As the band struck up the tune, he lit the cigar and dove into the song with reckless abandon. As the singing grew more furious, the stogie burned hotter and hotter until Mark's head was enveloped in a cloud of smoke. But with his fellow musicians laughing so hard they could barely keep the beat, he finished the last verse.

WHO WOULDN'T KNOW PASSION

By the late 1980s, David Miner—already well-known as one of the top bassists in Los Angeles—had his career as a producer also take off. As a result, there were recording executives who were interested in any project he put his hand to. As a long time friend of Mark Heard's, and a fan of his songwriting, David had often expressed interest in producing one of Mark's albums. Mark was without a label at the time, so he sent David a few demo tapes full of new songs. David liked what he heard, and he shopped the tapes around for a while. Unfortunately, there were no takers. The various producers who heard Mark's music agreed that the songwriting was fantastic, but they weren't interested in signing him because they didn't like the way he sang.

I was astounded when I first heard that story. What did they mean, *they didn't like the way he sang?* Any who have listened to Mark's albums or seen him perform know that he sang with more passion than almost any recording artist around. Indeed, that passion could produce an intensity bordering on ferocity. "When I listen to songs like 'Tip of My Tongue,'" Randy Stonehill comments, "it's almost like I can hear this guy's spirit trying to claw out through his rib cage."

Years after Mark's death, Buddy Miller recalled:

> You know it's funny. That [passion] was in everything he did, everything he sang. After I knew him a little bit from engineering his record, we [Julie and I] were working on Julie's second record for Word. There was a song on there that needed some backup vocals. We said, "Let's ask Mark." It was kind of a goofy song. It wasn't deep or heavy like Mark's: just a simple . . . rock song. We didn't realize it at the time that we're asking a guy who writes these heavy, deep, sometimes dark songs to sing on a song that would probably seem sort of bubble-gummish . . .

> I just remember him coming in [to our house where we recorded in a couple rooms] and going in there on this pop rock back-up part, and just giving it every ounce that was in him. The door was open between the two rooms, so we could see him, and it amazed us both how he turned what would be a pretty trivial part . . . into something a lot more intense than it was. It was eye opening for Julie and me. We still talk about it.

That intense passion brought something special to Mark's recordings, something more than his brilliant songwriting or his talent as a multi-instrument musician. It was something you wouldn't catch just by looking at his lyrics. You had to hear him sing to understand. Jim Scott, who helped produce Mark's final album, *Satellite Sky*, was amazed to watch him at work in his studio. "We had to make a big time record for small time money," he explains. "And it was great." Mark would be sitting behind the console with his headphones on, and he would (as Jim describes): "go the full distance. A performance every time. He gave it everything. That's what knocked me out."[8]

The last song Mark ever recorded was a rendition of the traditional hymn, "My Redeemer Lives," for the first *At the Foot of the Cross* project. When Jean Heard first heard that recording she was disturbed. Initially it seemed to her that the song lacked feeling. Later, however, when she had listened again, she realized that it didn't lack feeling at all; rather, it was infused with passion from start to end. The reason she hadn't heard little pieces of passion inserted here and there was because the passion was constant throughout.

Steve Hindalong described how he and Derri Daugherty got Mark involved in that project.

> Well we really wanted [Mark] to sing . . . "My Redeemer Lives." He was very resistant, saying, "Do you want me to sing the harmony, or something?"
>
> "No, we want you to sing the lead," [I insisted]. So I went over to his house [with some basic tracks already recorded]. He had a mobile [recording] truck where he worked. [It was a spare environment.] He would punch himself in. He didn't even have a remote. He wouldn't wear headphones. He'd have a microphone out by his console, and he'd lean over as far as he could, in this real awkward position, to punch himself in. Then he'd take four or five steps and sing.
>
> He did the thing in pretty much one pass. Punched himself in on a line or two. And really committed to that. And then that night we went and saw Pam Dwinell, who's now Kate Miner. We watched her sing in a club. We asked her back to sing the harmony. And then Mark mixed the song right there and then I took it back down to the guys.

On stage, Mark was infamous for spitting as he belted out his songs. His fans learned quickly not to sit in the front row at his concerts. Steve recalls the first time he saw Mark perform. "I was blown away because he screamed all the time. Every time he hit the chorus he just screamed."

"I loved watching him perform," Stonehill echoes. "There was an intensity and a kind of candor, an unabashed transparency about him, in a way. He really tried to dismiss the trappings of showbiz and just get up there and try to be real and in the moment."

Indeed, that passion and transparency ran through all aspects of his life, in ways both positive and negative. "I think all the people who were involved with Mark had moments when it was extremely frustrating dealing with his passionate side," comments Joel Russell, who was a close friend of the Heards, and spent many weeks on the road touring with Mark as an agent/road-manager. "Everything was right there on the surface for Mark."

Unfortunately, the recording industry had no category for passion. What was an asset to his fans was a liability to the industry folks. They didn't understand passion. It couldn't be labeled. It couldn't be packaged and marketed. So they rejected him.

IF IT SWALLOWED THEM WHOLE

When I reflect on this aspect of Mark Heard's life, his song "Big Wheels Roll" often comes to mind. Of course with Mark, as with any writer, it would be a mistake to assume autobiographical significance to the characters in his songs, even when he writes in the first person. Nonetheless, the more I've learned about Mark, the more I've felt that what he was sharing in this song was very much his own experience.

One of Mark's closest friends was Chuck Long. Indeed, if there was one common aspect to almost every interview I did for this book, it was that I needed to talk with Chuck. (The other name that kept coming up was Pat Terry, a.k.a. "Flippy the Fishhead.") Chuck and Pat both knew Mark from before he graduated from college, and their friendship with him lasted through the years. It was largely Chuck who financed the formation of Fingerprint Records and through it the recording of Mark's final three albums. In October of 2002, I finally connected with Chuck and Pat together, meeting at a hotel in Asheville, North Carolina. Partway through the interview, Chuck made a comment that confirmed some of what I'd been thinking about with respect to "Big Wheels Roll."

> I was intimately involved in the last three records. All of those songs are experiential for him. If you ever hear pain—like in the song "I Just Wanna Get Warm"—he was talking about himself. He was always writing from experience. I don't think he knew any

other way to do it.

A moment later, Chuck reaffirmed this thought. "All those songs you hear on those three albums are definitely him, and where he is in time and relationships and everything."

So where was Mark "in time and relationships" when he penned "Big Wheels Roll"? And how much of him do we see in the song's protagonist? At the start of the first verse we are struck with the character's desire to "make a dent on the shrinking world." Twenty years of disappointments have not altogether destroyed the hope that he might still accomplish something of value: that he might have some positive impact on the world through his life and his art. (Not insignificantly, Mark was approaching twenty years out of college when he recorded that song.) But even if those twenty years haven't erased all hope, they have left a bitter taste: a realization that "the pent-up way it works still stinks."

Then, too, there was the proverbial burning of the candle—or maybe the cigar—at both ends. All his activity could, at times, feel simply like the spinning of wheels in gravel: lots of noise but not much getting accomplished: no momentum, just something to keep him occupied: the busyness of subsistence—thoughts not unlike those expressed in the song "Nod Over Coffee."

Unfortunately, as Mark's character tells himself in the song, "associations can weaken one's place in history." It was not long into Mark's own career before he began to feel that his unintended association with the contemporary christian music industry and corresponding subculture was hurting his own career, and cutting into his ability to be taken seriously by the broader community.

But what of the music industry itself? What of the people who might have helped him? They disappeared, unwilling to "interfere" for fear of hurting their own careers. "Lame and weak," the song calls them. As Chuck commented, "I don't think Mark felt mistreated. [However] there were people whom he felt could have cut him some slack—I know that for a fact."

Yet the real problem of the music industry was not simply its selfishness and unwillingness to help. The real scathing indictment is in the last verse. They "wouldn't know passion if it swallowed them whole."

LEFT BRAIN RISK

There's that "passion" thing again. The shaking of fists and baring of one's soul. Of all Mark's many gifts, his passion was not the least. Unfortunately, the world—or at least the recording industry upon which Mark was dependent—did not know the value of passion. And so it went unnoticed by those who wouldn't have known it if it swallowed them whole.

Or worse. Maybe those who listened to Mark's demos did hear the passion, but they just couldn't label it and package it in a neat commercial box. And so it represented a threat, or at best a commercial liability: a left-brain risk: a needless myth that cooler heads (with a clearer sense of the value of money but no knowledge of love or passion or art) knew enough to stay away from.

So does this leave us with the view of Mark Heard as a martyr—somebody too good for the industry? That would be an easy and convenient approach. But as Chuck pointed out, even though there were some individuals whom Mark felt could have helped him, he did not by-and-large feel mistreated. Pat Terry agreed, "I think it is a little more multifaceted than that [simplistic answer]." Even the character in "Big Wheels Roll" ultimately fears that "he only has himself to blame."

To return to what I wrote in the preface, there were many reasons for Mark's lack of success, which include his own stubbornness, some bad luck and unfortunate timing, and also the fact that he really was "stuck in the middle"—he was too sacred for the sinners, but the saints often wished he would leave.[9] As Pat Terry said:

> There are a million reasons why Mark didn't have a major deal on a major label. Some of them had to do with the fact that it's a very commercial industry built on marketing, and Mark's music was not easily marketable. But it's also that people who hit the big deal in the music industry—their egos enable them to go out and demand a deal. Mark was not of that personality. There was also just timing and luck. There are a million things that come together to make people connect with a mainstream audience. We have to be careful with Mark. If you play too hard with the angle, "he was too good for the industry," it undermines how hard he worked and how much he wanted to compete and have his music taken seriously as part of the American music landscape.
>
> There have been plenty of other serious writers who were just

as esoteric and 'uncommercial' as Mark, but somehow, over time, they found their audience and got the opportunity to make their statement . . . artists like Bruce Springsteen . . . Bruce Cockburn . . . those kinds of writers. I think Mark wrote on that level of creativity and honesty. But time ran out. Mark wasn't disdainful about having a career and selling lots of records. He wanted to make that kind of statement, but he wanted to do it on his own terms. He felt trapped in the christian music thing that made people think of him in a way that he didn't think about himself.

[And yet] He accomplished more than most people ever will. People will know Mark Heard when they've forgotten many of the artists who were struggling to be heard during that time. And he made a real impact, developing a loyal audience even though he had to do it in an independent way.

I JUST WANNA GET WARM

1991, *Second Hand*

The mouths of the best poets
Speak but a few words
And then lay down
Stone cold in forgotten fields
Life goes on in this ant farm town
Cold to the lifeblood underfoot
All talk and no touch
And I just wanna be real
I just wanna be real

The colors here are monochrome
Studies in one shade of grey
The good times and the hard times
Cut from the same grey cloth
And all the fires that crackle here
Consume but do not burn
All light and no heat
And I just wanna get warm
I just wanna get warm

The days they rattle past me
Like a tunnel round a train
Landscapes and heartaches
I don't know what I feel
All I know is my condition
Is worse than I can tell

The small talk and the slow burn

And I just wanna be healed

I just wanna get well

There are things I should remember

But I have forgotten how

I'm all tied up with no time

Trying to do too much

And the thoughts that I've avoided

Are the ones I need right now

Like a warm wind and love's hand

I just wanna be touched

I just wanna be touched

I just wanna be real

I just wanna be well

I just wanna be healed

And I just wanna be warm

NO
1988, released posthumously on *High Noon*

I was a soldier, came home in tatters
I won the battles and lost the war
Now that I'm older it doesn't matter
Some lives are stolen
I'm just one more

No—don't ask me what I miss
Nobody likes to kiss and speak of failure
No—don't ask me what I've lost
You know I like to talk and I might tell you

I was a laugher, I was a lover
I was another in other times
Rain in my rafters is all you'll discover
You needn't bother to read my mind

No—don't ask me what I miss
Nobody likes to kiss and speak of failure
No—don't ask me what I've lost
You know I like to talk and I might tell you

I have this nightmare of glowing embers
Safe by the fireplace when I was five
And in the night air it makes me tremble
I still remember what love is like

No—don't ask me what I miss

Nobody likes to kiss and speak of failure

No—don't ask me what I've lost

You know I like to talk and I might tell you

I SAID THINGS
1987, previously unreleased

I had to lash out at someone

I guess I'm just insecure and loud-mouthed somehow

We live in a world filled up with

Personal bombs with shortened fuses, excuses

I said things I wish I had not said

I said things I did not have to say

I said things I wish I had not said

I said things

Whenever I feel the heat

I rattle and strike just like some kind of reptile—meanwhile,

It's too hard to say I'm sorry

Too easy to hope you'll never notice I'm hopeless

I said things I wish I had not said

I said things I did not have to say

I said things I wish I had not said

I said things

Cross me and I'm ignited

Little grey mushroom clouds in my heart; war-marks

Hold me and bleed this poison

Out of my veins so I can focus on us

I said things I wish I had not said

I said things I did not have to say

I said things I wish I had not said

I said things

TIP OF MY TONGUE

1992, *Satellite Sky*

There's an oasis in the heat of the day

There's a fire in the chill of night

A turnabout in circumstance makes each a hell in its own right

I been boxed-in in the lowlands, in the canyons that think

I been pushed to the brink of the precipice and dared not to blink

I been confounded in the whirlwind of what-if's and dreams

I been burned by the turning of the wind back upon my own flames

Knock the scales from my eyes

Knock the words from my lungs

I want to cry out

It's on the tip of my tongue

I've seen through the walls of this kingdom of dust

Felt the crucial revelation

But the broad streets of the heart and the day-to-day

meet at a blind intersection

I don't want to be lonely, I don't want to feel pain

I don't want to draw straws with the sons of Cain

You can take it as a prayer if you'll remember my name

You can take it as the penance of a profane saint

Knock the scales from my eyes

Knock the words from my lungs

I want to cry out

It's on the tip of my tongue

There's an oasis in the heat of the day

There's a fire in the chill of night

And when I know them both, I'll know your love

I will feel it in the twilight,

As circumstance comes crashing through my walls like a train

Or like a chorus from the mountains of the ocean floor,

Like the wind-burst of birdwings taking flight in a hard rain,

Or like a mad dog on the far side of Dante's Door

Knock the scales from my eyes

Knock the words from my lungs

I want to cry out

It's on the tip of my tongue

I'M AFRAID OF YOU

1988, previously unreleased

In the flash of headlights

Street rendezvous

When along comes night along comes you

You got your hair down like a smoking gun

You pull that trigger

Watch me run

Everybody is afraid of something else

And I'm afraid of you

Discount on passion

Ring up the sale with the cherry red of your fingernails

Pounce like a panther watch like a hawk

Try to overcome some underdog

Everybody is afraid of something else

And I'm afraid of you

I'm afraid of you

I'm afraid of you

Mind over matter brain over brawn

I'm overwhelmed and under-armed

I might feel some pity

I might lose my cool

But I will not be your careless fool

Everybody is afraid of something else

And I'm afraid of you

TAKING YOUR PICTURE

1987, previously unreleased

Love can only see what it wants to see

I see hair out of place

An angel's face

And I want just to capture the touch of your eyes

You know this camera can't tell no lies

Hold it—watch the birdie

I'm taking your picture

Oh I'm taking your picture

Hold the pose

There's the hint of a giggle

There's the trace of a tear

Your face tells a story I love to hear

And I want to remember every noun and verb

Every memory's worth about a thousand words

Hold it—watch the birdie

I'm taking your picture

Oh I'm taking your picture

Hold the pose

There's a flash in the background

From the Sunday Times

There's lines on your forehead

Tiny lines

And I want to remember

What I can't forget

Another year older and forever (deep) in your debt

Hold it—watch the birdie

I'm taking your picture

Oh I'm taking your picture

Hold the pose

{2}

LONELY MOON

"As brilliant of a wordsmith as Mark was, he knew that

the 'Language of Love' is not words but deeds.

As he sang in that song, the greater verbs truly do 'blister our lips.'

It was a language he struggled to speak every day."

–Matthew Dickerson

LOVE IS SO BLIND

1992, *Satellite Sky*

Scarlet is the color of her heart against the night
Prism of her innocence fracturing the light
She will take her stairwell down to dark and heartless streets
And spend her season singing songs to infidels and thieves
Love is so blind
It's so blind

Her eyes will meet the faces of the profane and the poor
And give to them the pearls she keeps behind her inner doors
She will speak the truth and she will ache and she will bleed
for the idiots who own the air the prophets have to breathe
Love is so blind
It's so blind

She is not the mystery they make her out to be
She calls them like she sees them—she sees unselfishly
The ears of those who listen can be callous or concerned
pity her naïveté or marvel at her worth
Love is so blind
It's so blind

FACES IN CABS

Mark Heard connected with people at many levels. As I researched this book, I heard several stories about him calling up friends (and even new acquaintances) and asking for their help at various times with various projects. From most accounts, he seemed to have a good memory of who had made him what offers of assistance, and he was not ashamed to call those persons up if a time arose that he could make use of their offers. Whether it was sitting at his console helping him engineer, or adding an instrument track or back-up vocal track on some particular song, or just banging on tin cans and car doors to get sound samples, he didn't think twice about recruiting people to volunteer their talents on his albums.

Buddy Miller, for example, not long after meeting Mark for the first time, casually mentioned that he might be able to help Mark out with recording if he ever needed it. Buddy admits it was one of those comments made only in passing. He was familiar with Mark's music, but they barely knew each other personally. Thus, although the offer was meant to be sincere, he didn't really expect a call. To Buddy's surprise, however, within just a couple weeks Mark was on the phone calling him up to invite him over to help engineer a new project.[10]

My experience with Mark was similar. I must confess that the day Mark contacted me about helping out with his book project I was as surprised as I was honored. Mark had read my first novel, and he knew my father was in the book business, but I didn't feel I knew him especially well. Yet I had made the offer of help, and he had remembered and accepted that offer.

It was not Mark's acceptance of help, however, but his giving of help that most people remember most. About a year and a half after Mark Heard died, I helped bring Pierce Pettis and Kate Miner (then known as Pam Dwinell-Miner) to New England for some concerts. At the time Pierce was recording with Wyndham Hill's High Street Records. He was booked for one gig at the University of Vermont in Burlington on a Friday evening, and another at Williams College in Western Massachusetts (about three and a half hours south of Burlington) on Saturday evening. At both concerts, Kate was doing an opening set of her own, and then singing backing vocals for Pierce. Just getting to hear Pierce and Kate perform (separately and together) was worth the labor of bringing them out. But my efforts also had a fringe benefit in that I was able to schedule Kate to do a Saturday afternoon gig at Middlebury College where I taught. In order to add a little name recognition to the event, Pierce also agreed to swing by en route from UVM to Williams to make a cameo appearance.

The Middlebury show was in an intimate (though awkwardly-shaped) student coffee-house called The Gamut Room. Of the fifty-five or so in attendance, no more than a handful had previously heard of Mark Heard. Pierce and Kate, however, had not only been close friends of Mark's; they were both on stage with him at Cornerstone the night of his heart attack. With that in mind—and since Mark had performed at Middlebury a few years earlier—I had billed the concert as a Mark Heard Tribute. Some time into the show Kate performed a pair of Mark's songs with Pierce backing her on guitar. After singing "House of Broken Dreams" and "Look Over Your Shoulder," she told a story about Mark that I've never forgotten.

The year before, there had been a memorial service for Mark in the Los Angeles area. At the service, guests had been invited to get up and say a few words about what Mark had meant to them. It began with a stream of dignitaries in the music world: luminary performers as well as a few industry bigwigs. Each stood and talked about what a great songwriter and musician Mark was, and about how much his presence would be missed, etc.

It was the testimonials that followed, however, that most moved Kate. For when all the famous people were done speaking, up stepped the local postal carrier who delivered the Heard's mail, and the butcher from down the street, and the girl at the corner store, and on and on. A steady stream of regular folk off the street—people who didn't necessarily care about Mark Heard as a songwriter but whose lives had been deeply touched by Mark Heard as a human being—paid him tribute.

From a mercenary or commercial perspective, these were people whom Mark had little to gain from befriending. They were not the people with whom he needed to schmooze in order to get ahead. They were simply fellow humans, whom Mark reached out to because that's what Mark was about. *"She will take her stairwell down to dark and heartless streets . . . / Love is so blind."*

FRACTURING THE LIGHT

I shared Kate's story with Tom Howard, a long time friend of Mark's and a fellow musician with whom Mark worked on various occasions. "He was very much like that." Tom responded. "He enjoyed people. He was interested in people. He had a real interest in what made them tick, and what animated their lives, and he found himself pursuing very disparate interests because of it: this rug-weaving he got into [and furniture making]. He was kind of an erstwhile craftsman."

"He had a way of connecting with people that was really special and genuine," recalls Mark's friend, one-time agent, and neighbor John Flynn. "That openness [was there]. His writing could be very much in the future, but [in his relationships] he was present most of the time."

John Austin, who began his career in Mark's studio in the fall of 1991 at the age of twenty-two, recording his debut CD *The Embarrassing Young*, recalls their first few meetings and brief days of recording together.

> I was struck by his friendly voice, but also by the way he seemed comfortable with silence, even on the phone. Most people I talked with seem to want to fill up the silence, or seize the silence as an opportunity to get off the line . . . but Mark, if he didn't really have something to add, just kept his mouth shut.

Though Mark could be quiet, he did spend a great deal of time talking with those closest to him: especially Chuck Long and Pat Terry early in his life. In his last few years, that circle expanded to include Dan Russell, who became, along with Chuck, Mark's business partner in the formation of Fingerprint Records. Dan recalls:

> Mark called me five days, if not seven days a week. He had a name he called me. It was a name a loving big brother would call his younger brother. The tone of his voice, the name itself, conveyed love and encouragement.

Another way Mark connected with people was on the level of his humor, which was notorious, though rarely (if ever) mean-spirited. On one occasion, Mark went with Bono (of U2) to a concert of The Budapest Women's Quartet. During the concert, he started teasing Bono for his lack of vocal range after noticing him sitting with his mouth open, trying (unsuccessfully) to reach the low notes that the women were hitting.[11]

John Austin also remembers seeing Mark's sense of humor come out at a Cornerstone Festival a couple years before he died. Every now and then a fan would come by and ask if they could take his picture. Mark would comply with the request, but as soon as they were done he'd ask if he could take a picture of them with *their* camera. They seemed a little confused, but went along with it. "In the time I stood there, I saw this happen twice. The second time I saw it, I started catching the trickster humor in it." When asked for an autograph, Mark also signed his name backwards.

"He was a tremendous mimic," Tom Howard added. "He could mimic people spot on—never with any kind of rancor. He enjoyed the mannerisms of people. He took it in and he could give it out. He had an imitation of me that was hilarious. Sounded just like me."

Having heard much of Mark's generosity as well as his craftsmanship, I was not surprised when I learned from Jean Heard that Mark had been a Boy Scout in his youth and had earned the prestigious advanced rank of Eagle Scout. Indeed, everybody I spoke with who knew Mark well had some memory of him giving of himself to help or encourage others, usually with no thought of personal gain. If there was ever a time when this generous spirit might have been put to the test, it would have been when Mark's younger sister Susan totaled his car the summer before his junior year of college, and her freshman year. As might be expected of any young sister, Susan was not looking forward to telling her brother what had happened to his car after the accident. "When I got back home I was apprehensive that he might be angry, but he never mentioned the fact that I had wrecked his car, just said that he was glad I wasn't hurt."

Susan also described Mark's thoughtfulness in his approach to giving gifts. He would find gifts that were both personal—an indication that he took the time to know the interests of people to whom he gave the gifts— and artistic. "He always seemed to pick gifts for everyone that symbolized something special. One of his last gifts to me was a bracelet. He knew I liked silver flatware, and was at a craft fair where someone was making a bracelet from a fork."

As a married couple, hospitality was one big part of the Heard's generosity. It seems that at times the Heard's little two-bedroom house was like a hotel for friends who were moving to Los Angeles and needed a place to stay for a while until they got settled—guests who often stayed for weeks or even months at a time. At one point, with Tim Alderson already living in Mark and Janet's only guestroom, John Flynn moved in also.

> I told them I was thinking of coming out to California, and at the time Mark had just started his studio. It was probably just conversation, but to me it was like a job offer. Basically he

was saying, "Hey, maybe we could use you as an assistant in my studio." So I considered that a job offer, and they offered to let me stay there for a month while I got settled.

Of course when Mark felt it was time for John to go, he let him know without too much concern for diplomacy. Years later, John smiles at the memory of the night Mark "threw him out of the house."

> On the thirtieth day [after I moved in], Mark said, "So when are you planning on moving out or getting a place of your own?" That was kind of a pivotal moment because it was fairly abrupt and it just kind of came out of the blue. My feelings at the time were probably a little hurt and so forth, but it would be two days later and he would call me up and say, "Hey, why don't you come over for dinner?"

> That's just how he related. Everything was right there, and he would just say what he felt, and it didn't always come out the best way. There were a lot of those little moments when he would get frustrated with me, or he'd get mad at me, or he'd get mad at a situation. Then later he would come back and make sure I knew that it really wasn't that he didn't like me or didn't care for me; it was just the moment.

SHE GIVES TO THEM THE PEARLS

As Buddy Miller got to know Mark a little better, he became impressed with how vulnerable Mark's unselfish giving could be. One particular instance came to his mind right away.

> Victoria Williams got sick with M.S.—she and [my wife] Julie were best friends—and Marvin Etzioni organized a benefit for her. And I thought this is a cool thing, and I love Mark's records, and there's always accordion on all his records, and Julie had been using accordion on her records, and we were going to do a set together. So I thought "Let's ask Mark if he wants to do accordion." It's a neat event—a nice hang—and T Bone [Burnett] and Sam [Phillips] (whom we didn't know but Mark knew) would be there. So we asked Mark to play, and Mark hesitated, and then said "Okay." But then he added, "I don't really play accordion." I thought he was just being humble, but apparently he didn't really

play. He just punched in a lot when he recorded. But he came down nonetheless, and did a great job.

Pierce Pettis and Randy Stonehill recalled different ways Mark demonstrated his care for them while in the studio engineering and producing their albums. For Pierce, it was Mark's unflagging labor and devotion to the *Tinseltown* project, even when he was so laid up with what turned out to be lactose intolerance that he had to run the recording console while lying down on a couch.

John Austin told me another interesting story about Mark's work on that album.

> Mark was friends with T-Bone Burnett, and passed up an opportunity to go hang out with Bob Dylan because he was working with Pierce on his record. When Pierce said, "You should go," Mark said "Who is Bob Dylan? He is some guy named Robert Zimmerman, and I have work to do.

Some of Mark's response may well have come from a refusal to buy into celebrity culture. "He didn't believe the myth," John added. "He didn't have time for it. He was doing some serious work." But some of Mark's response must surely have come from his commitment to Pierce and to the project Pierce was working on.

For Randy Stonehill, it was more Mark's patience and gentleness that demonstrated his respect and affection. They were working long hours on *Return to Paradise*. Randy would be struggling with some difficult guitar parts, "fighting with his own ghosts" as he described it. He would feel his concentration start to flag, as he heard the little voices in him telling him he wasn't good enough. "And here was [Mark] working hard, putting in long hours. His job was to be an engineer, not a therapist. But he never said 'Randy, we're burning daylight here, so just suck it up.'"

Randy saw two things at work here. Part of it was just Mark's wisdom in wanting him to be comfortable in order to deliver his best. But Randy also always felt that it was Mark's unspoken way of saying he cared about him and understood what he was going through. In Randy's mind, Mark was saying, through his actions: "I want this project to be good, not just so that we get it done and I get my payday, but because I want you to be the best you can be."

"One of the most special memories of my whole relationship with him,"

Randy remembers, "was just how he was so gracious and giving in the midst of my personal struggles. And because of that, I ended up delivering probably one of the most authentic performances [I have ever given] on record."

One of the few handwritten letters I ever received from Mark—the rest were all typed—was a letter of encouragement regarding my own writing. It was penned on September 20, 1987, at a time before my first novel had been published, when all I was receiving from publishers were rejection letters. Though he had only met me twice, and I was completely unknown as a writer, Mark had taken the time to read (and comment on) some of my unpublished short stories, and to suggest some connections between my work and that of other authors whom he liked. That letter, from a songwriter whose works I appreciated more than any other, was certainly a factor in helping me continue to write and not to lose heart.

It was not until much later that I realized just how generous and selfless his action was, even beyond the gift of his time. For, in addition to his thoughts on my story, the letter also contained the brief comment, "Can't say . . . what all will happen next for me. *Tribal Opera* didn't do as well as we had hoped. I'm cutting new demos now, but don't know what [the] label situation will end up being." Though it was a time of great uncertainty and discouragement for Mark, the focus of his letter was not on his own problems but on encouraging a young artist.

I learned I was not the only one who benefited from Mark's encouraging words. Even when life was most difficult for him, he made the effort to lift others. As mentioned earlier, Mark's friendship with Pat Terry started in the early-mid 1970s when Mark was still in College. In the early 1980s, Mark ended up producing three albums for Pat:

> When I got to know Mark, I was already recording, and my path took me along a more mainstream christian music kind of path in the '70s—the Pat Terry Group—and I think Mark, because we were friends, he understood what we were doing, but I'm not sure it was where he wanted to be and I'm sure there were elements of it he didn't respect.

> We were friends and got along fine and stayed in touch on and off through the years. At the end of that period, about 1979, philosophically I was having problems with some of the elements of that and I felt like hopefully I was maturing and growing up a

little bit, and disbanded the group. I was pretty frazzled at that time of my life and trying to figure out what does it mean to be a Christian person and to be an artist—a musician and a writer. And Mark and I connected in a fresh way at that time, and he was so encouraging and supportive at that time. I still have letters he wrote in which he said, "Just because you're getting resistance from people doesn't mean you're not asking the right questions. Don't get discouraged with this." And he came by the house and listened to new songs I wrote and was very encouraging. I really credit Mark at that time of life in keeping me from throwing up my hands and giving up. He was really very generous at that point with me.

On a similar vein, Phil Madeira shared with me, "I still have many letters that Mark wrote to Elinor and me. He was very encouraging to me as an artist, and very meticulous in commenting about what he felt the strengths were in what I was doing at the time."

APPALACHIAN MELODY

So what brought this compassionate Georgia boy to Los Angeles in the first place? It had not been his original plan to move to the West Coast. In 1976, Mark was still single and living in Atlanta, looking for a job that would provide the financial security so that he could ask Janet Currin—his sweetheart of three years—to marry him. Seeking an opening in the music business, he traveled to Indiana to a national gathering of artists and industry people in the newly growing contemporary christian music sub-culture.

Featured at this meeting were Larry Norman and Randy Stonehill, two of the best known artists in the genre. Indeed, at the time they were among only a small handful of national recognized names in a christian music business that was just beginning to take off. Larry had formed Solid Rock Records, which had released his own album *In Another Land*, as well as Randy's *Welcome to Paradise*. The two had come to the conference to perform, and to talk about songwriting. They had also come, in part, just to encourage younger artists who were exploring songwriting or looking for record deals.

As Randy would later realize and confess, the two of them had a certain arrogance at the time. Convinced that they were the "young turks" on the cutting edge—which in certain respects was true—they assumed that they had a lot more to give than to receive. So there they were, standing in the lunch line, when up came this "shy Georgia boy with too much curly brown hair." He gingerly asked if he might come by their cabin later and play a few songs. Larry and Randy condescended to allow him to sing for them, not really expecting much. Some time later, Mark appeared outside their cabin. The memory is still vivid for Randy.

> I'll never forget Mark coming to the cabin, and sitting on this wooden fence on the front porch with this sort of golden movie-set light of late afternoon behind him, and these leaves sort of gently drifting down from the trees. Larry and I sat in these two chairs in front of him, and then just watched and listened in kind of amazement as he played "Castaway." And I just knew that we'd found a treasure.

> Mark was concentrating on a song, and I think he kind of had his eyes shut. He was singing and playing. And I just looked at Larry and he looked at me, our eyes got wide and we kind of nodded at each other, like "Listen to this guy. Man. Eureka! We've found it."

Mark was soon offered a recording contract with Solid Rock. Shortly after, on April 2, 1977, he and Janet married—Janet's father mistakenly assuming that the record contract meant that Mark would have some sort of financial security to support a wife!

The permanent move to Los Angeles did not come immediately, however. Both Mark and Janet had family roots in Georgia. The plan was just to fly out to Los Angeles to do the recordings, and then to return home. In November of 1977 they made the trip. What they soon learned, however, was that Larry was not prepared to just bring Mark into the studio, spend the necessary time (and money) to record an album, and then send him home. The album would be recorded in bits and pieces over several months, whenever Larry had time to work on it. Unfortunately, these periods of work were often weeks or months apart. And Mark needed to be ready whenever the opportunity arose. So in March of 1978 they moved to L.A. and made it their home.

"It was shortly thereafter," Randy continued, "that I got the distinct impression that I was in the presence of greatness . . . that it was special that he was in my life. I wanted him to have more and more involvement in my work, and I starting thinking to myself, 'Why is it that I like Mark Heard's recordings better than my own, which are done on three times the budget?'"

SHAKING
1989, previously unreleased

She was a little girl from far away who came to stay

She lives out East a way

Beyond the city haze

They say she's long and fair

With Summer flowers in her hair

She bears the lovely name

Of some Ancient Spanish saint

You don't wanna know her

Or get on her bad side

You don't want her to come looking for you

If you value your life

She'll have you SHAKING

You don't wanna go feel her touch

SHAKING Rocking and reeling and all shook up

SHAKING A kind of passion that's just too much

SHAKING You don't wanna go SHAKING

The girl has got her faults

She sleeps a lot and that's not all

Every now and then

She comes looking for a wild time

Though she's the quiet sort

When she cuts loose she can't be stopped

She's a match for any chap

Who's dumb enough to try

If she comes to see you
You'd best be out of town
She'll jolt you with her sweet caress
And spin your world around

[CHORUS]

She'll shake the teeth from your skeleton
Shake your house from its foundation
When she walks on your shattered peace
She leaves her footprints size 8.3

When she comes to town
The place she walks is holy ground
At about the speed of sound
She'll have you on your knees
Well she don't mean no harm
When she takes you in her loving arms
But when she's spent her charm
You'll never be the same

If you want a permanent memory
Of a moment in your life
Just meet her in a high-rise
And hang on for your life

DEEP WATER (IN THE WELL OF A MEMORY)

1987, previously unreleased

I'm nothing but king of the nightshift

Got nothing but time

Have nothing but perfume and warships on my mind

My memory swells like a beesting

What have I become

My tangles with love and with war have left me numb, so numb

Deep water in the well of a memory

Deep water in the well

Deep water in the well of a memory

Sweet souvenirs and keepsakes of hell

Got me a confused recollection

For when I was young

No tears of my own could corrode the copper sun

But her kiss was a flammable vapor

And I got myself burned

Left me with these fire-eater's scars inside my lungs, so young

Deep water in the well of a memory

Deep water in the well

Deep water in the well of a memory

Sweet souvenirs and keepsakes of hell

My brother his grave's on the high seas

Whitewater and flame

He mighta got out in a lifeboat same as me

Now I'm nothing but king of the nightshift

No warriors to slay

Just outrunning my conscience and living to tell the tale, time will tell

Deep water in the well of a memory

Deep water in the well

Deep water in the well of a memory

Sweet souvenirs and keepsakes of hell

SHE'S A BIG DREAMER
1988, previously unreleased

She moves her eyes like a Summer sun

And hopes that the planets are following

Like she could change their orbits with a honeyed thumb

She's a big dreamer

She's a hot June breeze in the Wintertime

But no icicles are trickling

Like she could talk all clocks out of keeping time

She's a big dreamer

> She's a big dreamer

> She's a big dreamer

She's an angel's dream with her flaxen locks

And hopes all dozers are noticing

Like she could hold their hearts in a hammer lock

She's a big dreamer

She parts her lips with the greatest poise

And hopes young misters are listening

Like she could shatter their ears with the slightest noise

She's a big dreamer

She's a big dreamer

She's a big dreamer

When the sun shines baby she's a bullet train

Riding on her own electricity

But when the cold wind blows she's a weathervane

She's a big dreamer

She's looking for love in a neon world

Same as the best of the rest of us

She's just a kicked around small town little girl

But she's a big dreamer

She's a big dreamer

She's a big dreamer

LANGUAGE OF LOVE

1992, *Satellite Sky*

What's happened to me

I look into my loved ones' faces

This skeleton key can't open up their secret places

I spend a feverish night deciding what I'll say

But words are not enough to carry days

All around the world it's the same thing

All around the world it's the blood in the words

All around the world

Same pages

Trying to speak the language of love

What's happened to me

I'm walking in the bones of a mortal

The message is brief but I'm talking like there's no tomorrow

I don't believe in cinematic confessional scripts

I find the greater verbs blister my lips

All around the world it's the same thing

All around the world it's the blood in the words

All around the world

Same pages

Trying to speak the language of love

Up against the tide of unjust years

Sentimental whispers seem to lose their meaning

What's happened to me

I look into my loved ones' faces

What matters to me

What matters in the four-walled spaces

I beg my flesh and bone to carry all I feel

A whirling wheel that words cannot conceal

All around the world it's the same thing

All around the world it's the blood in the words

All around the world

Same pages

Trying to speak the language of love

PERSUASION

1988, previously unreleased

I don't know what love is

I only know that I can see past my own complaints (mistakes)

Like a part of some cycle

Like a part of some bad gambler's blackjack game

That I'm losing

'Cause I can't get through to you

When the weight of my words comes crashing down

And if the words ain't true to you

Why don't you dance with me anyhow

If I can't persuade you

What kind of persuasion do you want

I don't have no brainchild

I just got some room in my heart for you

And like a typical juvenile

I got plenty of skin for my own tattoo

Your name in blue

And when I speak to you

I feel like the heir of a millionaire

And if that seems cheap to you

How about spend some time with me anyhow

If I can't persuade you

What kind of persuasion do you want

I can't get through to you

When the weight of my words comes crashing down

And if the words ain't true to you

Why don't you dance with me anyhow

If I can't persuade you

What kind of persuasion do you want

SECOND CHANCE

1988, previously unreleased

There is a landscape full of bleached bones

And I have been here once before

I'm here once more

It is the land of desperation

It is the heap of shattered dreams

Where fools come clean

What kind of fool have I become

One mistake is never enough

Some fool I am

Why did I have to go and wreck a second chance

When I first laid eyes upon you

There was a band of violins

You could not hear

It was just my admiration

But now it's just the paradox

That scares you off

What kind of fool have I become

One mistake is never enough

Some fool I am

Why did I have to go and wreck a second chance

I thought that we might talk it over

I said that we could work it out

Me and my big mouth

I feel a shock wave in the concrete

My shoes are full of prickly heat

You laugh I bleed

What kind of fool have I become

One mistake is never enough

Some fool I am

Why did I have to go and wreck a second chance

[Mark Heard, L'Abri, Switzerland]

{3}

AT THE MERCY OF THE FLAME

"You cannot underestimate the power of growing up in Macon,

Georgia on Mark: how Southern it was, and what-all came with that.

There was a wealth of characters . . . Those guys [who worked for his

dad] were amazing storytellers themselves, and also were subjects of

stories that Mark would tell. I think there was a pretty rich thread

running through his life of growing up in Macon . . .

I hear a lot of that, especially in that older stuff."

–Pat Terry

SHE DON'T HAVE A CLUE

1991, *Second Hand*

She's got smart-bomb eyes but they see no wrong

She don't understand there's a war going on

Melt my heart like lead—she got no X-ray sight

She says a day's a day and a night's a night

She don't see no blinding flashes

Says why don't I hold her hand

She don't have a clue

But she's mine

She is love, love, love

Say she must be mad, the girl has got no nerves

Never throws no stones, knows no dirty words

She will stumble on something good to say

In the darkest scene of your darkest day

She don't feel no threat in living

Asks if I've got a kiss to give her

She don't have a clue

But she's mine

Says "I am what I am"

She doesn't seem to dream,

hears no distant drums

Says I worry too much,

thinks I'm just plain glum

She doesn't lie awake, doesn't feel no rain

She's the only one that I know who's sane

She don't hear no shells exploding

Says why don't I hold her closer

She don't have a clue

But she's mine

She is love, love, love

Says "I am what I am"

EMOTIONAL MAN

Mark Heard and Janet Currin met in Ithaca, New York at a summer conference for college students run by Campus Crusade for Christ. Mark was a college senior at the time, and Janet a sophomore. Both were shy, but both being from Georgia they ended up driving home together at the end of the summer. Their relationship moved to a steady correspondence when Mark went back to school at the University of Georgia. Janet remembers receiving letters from Mark. They were so special that she wouldn't read them right away. She would hop on her bicycle and ride out to a small park. Then she'd climb up in a tree, and—sitting in the branches—would open his letters and pore over them.

A few years ago I was driving some Middlebury College students on a four-hour car trip across New England. I had the album *Second Hand* playing in the tape deck, and the song "She Don't Have a Clue" came on. I've always thought of it as a great love song in praise of a woman who—despite her wisdom in many areas of life: her ability to "stumble on something good to say in the darkest scene of your darkest day"—is nonetheless clueless when it comes to evil. Her smart-bomb eyes see no wrong. She doesn't understand war. She doesn't know any dirty words. The female students in the car with me, however, hearing only the chorus "she don't have a clue, but she's mine," and missing the context, were offended. They did not hear it as a sentimental song of praise.

I tentatively mentioned that song to Janet and wondered if he'd written it for her. "It's me," she admitted at once, with something of a shy smile. "He claimed that song was not about me, but I know it's me. I have to be honest about it. It's true." She didn't seem proud of this, but neither was she embarrassed. "It wasn't a negative thing. I would never take it as a negative thing."

As I considered Janet's response, and those of the female students who were in my car, it dawned on me that most of the songs I think of as Mark's best love songs are not always easily identifiable to the casual listener as "love songs." Indeed—perhaps in part because of Mark's passion and intensity—people often altogether missed his gentle and sentimental side, or his humorous side. Tom Howard was one who had a chance to see what he referred to as his "absolutely sentimental sweetness":

I remember the sentimental side. When Dori and I first got

married, Mark [and] Janet [also had] a young marriage going. Janet for the very first time since their marriage was going to take a trip by herself and visit her parents in Georgia (or wherever it was). She was going to be gone a week, and Mark could not stand the idea of going home to his house by himself, and so he asked to come and stay at our house—at our apartment in Pasadena. We said, "Sure. Whatever." He was very very somber and at one point I remember walking into the living room and he was sitting there by himself sobbing. I said, "Mark is there anything I can do for you?" and he said "No, I'm fine." I had the presence of mind to take Dori and leave and let him have his space. He was absolutely devastated that she was not physically present. And I think throughout the life of their marriage he was extremely connected with her.

Another time, when I first started doing these piano records, Mark was so supportive because he was really at that place in his life where he was seeing the seamy side of the christian music industry and he saw me doing these instrumental records (piano solos, and so forth) as kind of an out for me: like I was launching out into the bigger world. He came to that same apartment that we lived in, in Pasadena, one evening. Janet and he came for dinner. And we stood out on the porch in front, and I remember this to this day. It was so sweet and so caring because he said, "I want to tell you I'm really happy for you that you're doing this." He said "May God just take this and . . . " then he almost pronounced like a blessing. It turned into this very sweet benediction on my activities and what I was doing. I remember that to this day. I remember the look in his eyes. I don't think I've ever felt as connected just on a purely friendship level with him before or after that very evening with him. It bespoke a care and a depth to Mark that I think sometimes only came out with his closest friends—with Janet—and in his music.

Dan Russell commented that early in Mark's career, he often refused to travel without Janet; it was his condition for accepting a gig.

Oddly enough, for all his depth and insight as a songwriter, it was the simpler side to Mark's music that initiated many of his fans. Steve Hindalong commented:

The best time I ever had with Mark was in Switzerland when we went on this Europe trip. We had three weeks. We got Eurail passes. He'd been to L'Abri, so he was like our tour guide. He took us to meet Edith Schaeffer. He was extremely happy for that whole week in Switzerland. He took us up the Gondolas . . . There's nothing like it . . . We just sat there and listened to cowbells. Nothing else around for miles. Mark just sat there and smoked his pipe. That's the happiest I've ever seen him was that week. I loved that moment.

When you consider the complexity of much of Mark's music, that sentimental simplicity was even more astounding. Should I have been surprised when I learned that Mark was a fan of the show *All Things Great And Small?* In his earlier days of recording, this love of simple things was evident in songs like "Appalachian Melody" or "Moonflower." Though less obvious in his final three albums, one can still get the same picture. You can hear it in "All Too Soon," or even "Why, Mama Why," although in most of his later songs the sentimental simplicity most often came mixed with a deep sense of longing.

"I just think of those sweet moments at the end of those long days of recording," Randy Stonehill recollects. "We would sit in his broken down lawn furniture outside the mobile truck and stare up at the stars and he'd be talking about the space program. He was [equally] fascinated with just the Heavens as with the wonders of technology . . . sentimental about the beauty of the stars, and then very clinical about how these machines work."

THE EYE OF THE STORM

In fact, Mark's ability to capture in song something of that simple beauty, particularly in his acoustic music, was the source of a certain amount of tension in his musical career. Fans of Mark's early album, *Appalachian Melody*, kept hoping for another similar recording. Mark, however, was moving steadily from that early "folksy" approach to a more straight-ahead rock-and-roll sound: a sound that was both more interesting to him musically at the time, and also a better vehicle (he felt) for the things he wanted to express.

After the release of the much rockier *Victims of the Age* and *Stop the Dominoes*, there was pressure on Mark to record another acoustic album. It was a difficult time for Mark. He was under contract to Chris Christian's

Home Sweet Home label. Chris claimed that he had funded Mark's records at a time when nobody else would, and that he had lost a considerable amount of money doing so. However Home Sweet Home was making enough money off some of their other artists, most notably Amy Grant, that he could afford to continue working with Mark. In Chris's words, he wanted to "take Mark Heard's creativity and present it to the public. Mark was writing and recording very different music. It was not in the mainstream." At an artistic and spiritual level, Chris said he believed in what Mark was trying to do. Yet Chris was also a businessman. "I knew I probably wouldn't sell many records," he said, "but I wanted to give Mark a chance. Mark said things that make people stop and think: 'I wonder if I should reconsider this.'"

As for Mark, it may have been true that Chris's funding had enabled him to record some albums he might not otherwise have recorded (at least not immediately), but he hated being trapped. For one, he was trapped financially, having signed contracts that returned very little money to him. He was also trapped in a subculture; one reason he had signed with Home Sweet Home was that he had been led to believe his albums would be released in the general mainstream market, and not just in the contemporary christian sub-culture market. As much as anything, though, Mark was trapped because he wanted to move on both lyrically and musically. As Dan Russell commented, Mark:

> . . . signed with Chris Christian's Home Sweet Home because he was promised first and foremost, mainstream release, distribution, and promotion. That obviously didn't happen and he was locked into a multi-year recording agreement that netted him heartache, frustration, and depression.

And so, although Mark retained a friendship with Chris on a personal level, he was resentful of Home Sweet Home as a business and label: the symbol of an industry that he had little good to say about. As Mark's close friend Tim Alderson described it, "Mark genuinely liked Chris and they got along as friends, but every business deal they had Mark wanted to kill him."

In the end, Mark conceded to recording another acoustic album. "I didn't force him to do that acoustic album," Chris defends, "But I did ask him [to do it]. He was gracious enough to say, 'I think I can do it. Let me go work on it. It's not what I'd like to do next, but I can do it.'"

In the process, both Chris and Mark felt as though they were doing each other a favor. Mark thought he was doing a favor for Chris by giving him an "extra" record that would make money for his company. Chris perceived that he was doing Mark a favor; nudging him in the direction that would not only bring some financial success, but which would bring his music to the greatest number of people. Nearly twenty years later, Chris still says, "He was the greatest artist I've ever worked with." And in the same breath, he adds, "All I've done is support him financially."

The result of their agreement was the 1983 release *Eye of the Storm*, Mark's most acoustic project to date: a sort of *Appalachian Melody: Part 2*. But the album came with the strange note on the jacket: "This album is a special one-time release of acoustic guitar-oriented material." It was as if Mark was warning everybody not to expect anything like that again.

The problem—as well as the irony of the situation—was that the album, which Mark hadn't even wanted to make in the first place, sold really well. Even many of Mark's musician friends appreciated its simple beauty. And so, of course, Chris immediately wanted Mark to do another album just like it. Mark, on the other hand, had no desire to make another. The whole project had been a favor for Chris, and not something that had come from where he was musically at the time. Yet Mark was still under contract, and so now he was feeling even more trapped.

Pat Terry seemed to have a good take on what was going on with Mark and why he was resistant.

> Some of it was simply because I think Mark may have equated these acoustic records with a more mainstream contemporary christian music thing which he really did not want to be a part of. We used to talk and I would say, "It's still your music. Write the songs you want, but do them on an acoustic guitar and call it a record."

> But I think with him the struggle was a kind of a guilt-by-association because he had so many issues with the whole concept of contemporary christian music that he didn't want to be lumped in with that. He saw himself as a Christian person who was a musician rather than a person who was making "christian music." So he found himself in a situation where the labels he was working with were "christian labels"; the concerts he was performing were sponsored by "christian organizations"; and he

was actually trying to accomplish something in that realm that, frankly, didn't have much to do with what that was about. So he was constantly banging his head against the wall (figuratively) over these kind of issues.

So he was thinking, "I want to be making rock-and-roll records that don't get lumped into that." And that's why it was so frustrating for him to be pressured to do those things.

THE ASHES AND THE DUST

In any case, Mark did go on to record two more albums for Home Sweet Home. The first of these, *Mosaics,* was the album Mark wanted to do. If viewed in the context of the contemporary christian music scene, it was *avant-garde* for its time: much less folksy than *Eye of the Storm.* In fact, it was a big departure from his earlier acoustic material and the singer-songwriter sorts of ballads he had often recorded. So much so that Home Sweet Home sat on *Mosaics* and didn't release it right away. Instead, Chris made yet another deal with Mark to record yet another more traditional and acoustic album, *Ashes and Light.*

Again, as Tim Alderson describes:

> *Mosaics* is the one that Mark wanted to make. *Ashes and Light* he felt compelled to make, and he was so unhappy. I mean, he was just miserable. In fact, he took part of his recording budget and flew Pat Terry out here so that Pat could hang out with him just to keep him from going insane and shooting himself. And Pat was a really good influence on Mark because Pat had all the same frustrations with the christian music business that Mark did, but Pat's personality was such that he had a better disposition for dealing with stress.

"I was comic relief," Pat explains. "[Mark] was really frustrated . . . so he flew me out there and I just sat in the control room and made funny noises."

Pat did have one particular memory of the recording of *Ashes and Light,* and how Mark carried out his rebellion even in his reluctant agreement to record.

> My one memory of *Ashes and Light* was that he was a song short for the record. So one night after dinner he said "Come in

here and write a song with me because we've got to have another song for this thing." So we wrote "Threw it Away" together. And I remember arguing with him about the word "atrophy." He wanted to use the word atrophy. And we got to the point and I said, "Atrophy is so unmusical and it sounds so clinical." And he wouldn't even talk with me about it. I said, "I don't think that's the word" and he said [very bluntly] "That's the word" and he got very clipped.

I always interpreted this as follows: that he wanted to choose that word because it was such an un-contemporary-christian-music kind of word. Some of this is speculation, but knowing his mindset there, there was definitely an attitude of "I'm going to make this record but it's going to be on my terms." It was very calculated.

Pat laughs at the memory. "I still think it's the wrong word," he says. I also laughed when I heard that story, remembering that in another song ("Straw Men") on the same album, Mark used the phrase 'pious anhedonia.' When I first heard that song, I had to look up the word anhedonia.[12] And it wasn't even *in* the *first* dictionary I checked! (Even now, my spell-checker doesn't even have the word.) In any case, whether those words are right or wrong poetically is not the central issue from the point of view of this book. If Mark couldn't establish his independence from the subculture through the musical style, then he would do it through his choice of vocabulary.

Unfortunately, the effect on Mark of what he felt—pressure to fit a mold, was not especially humorous. And the tension that Mark already felt was exacerbated when Chris released *Ashes* before *Mosaics*, even though *Ashes* was recorded later and *Mosaics* was the album Mark had wanted to do. In the process, Mark ended up even more bitter and frustrated with the entire deal. Not surprisingly, he never cared much for either *Eye of the Storm* or *Ashes and Light*, and he would rarely perform any of that material in concert. In fact, he quickly put that whole era of his career behind him, and tried not to look back! But it didn't take much to see the bad taste it had left in his mouth.

To that end, some of the recollections of fellow songwriter Bill Mallonee (of the Vigilantes of Love) are very telling. Bill and Mark didn't meet until late in Mark's life, but their acquaintance (however brief) held the intensity that comes from working very closely together on a project of great importance to both of them. As I was working on this book, Bill shared with me some memories of and reflections on that time. At his request, I quote his letter to me in its entirety:

I only knew Mark about two weeks, [and] had no real familiarity with him before that. I'd heard a few of his acoustic-type records and thought they were sort of a Christian James Taylor, and I was almost completely unaware of this animal known as Contemporary Christian Music, where Mark had made some sizable inroads. So initially I didn't want him involved with *Killing Floor*, Vigilantes of Love's third release. But he sorta came with the Fingerprint package. And after I heard the stellar songs and mixing on Mark's *Satellite Sky*, I realized he was indeed a fabulous songwriter, performer and a very organic producer—just what I was looking for. I was won over as they say!

When I first met Mark he had just pulled into Athens, GA. We would spend the next two weeks recording the album with John Keane, Peter Buck of R.E.M., and Mark Maxwell. When I met Mark [Heard], he was pretty depressed, sullen, and reserved; he seemed pretty beat-up by dynamics that maybe I came to understand later. Some of those battles and such I came to understand personally as my own career took off and others I grasped as I learned more about Mark after his death. It's hard to get to know someone as quiet as he was. I frequently had [the] other two Fingerprint Record's owners, Dan Russell and Chuck Long, fill me in on his past: Mark's struggle to forge a new musical identity; his battle [to] gain some acceptance for music that [had] grown far afield from that ghetto known as Contemporary Christian Music; and of course the recent and sudden death of his father. All of this weighed heavily on Mark like some mantle of doom. His health problems were stress and anxiety related.

You could tell, upon retrospect, that here was a deep-feeling and sensitive man, but one crushed by his circumstances and who was burning both ends of an invisible candle. Still, Mark loved the songs I'd written and was now playing, and he impressed everyone with his engineering and production talents. Keane, Maxwell, and Pete Buck were all verbal and complimentary towards his ideas and energy in the studio. Me? I was just glad to be getting down a record that felt like a piece of me in every way, with a lot of different facets, and Mark did what a good producer should always attempt to do: he brought out the best in me.

I remember Pete Buck turning to Mark (Heard) after he heard the final mixes for "Real Downtown" (clearly an R.E.M. influenced tune!), and saying to [him], "Well, that was great! I guess we need to discuss co-producer credits!" See, up until that point I think it was assumed that Pete would be the producer, and Mark the engineer. Now this is the sorta stuff that means very little to most fans and record buyers, BUT for those who spend a lot of their lives parked in front of near field speakers listening to playback after playback, a production credit is a type of validation. It's a pat on the back and a raised glass to those long hours and hard work of trying to bring a vision to fruition. I think Pete's comment was great validation to Mark. Here was a fella (Pete Buck, R.E.M.'s gifted guitar player and songwriter) that was at the top of his game. The band had become international pop stars with the hit, "Losing My Religion," and Peter, the writer of that song, was complimenting Mark, whom he'd never heard of, on the great quality of his work.

I have one more memory (a sad one) of an incident with Mark, and it runs like this: Mark was just getting ready to leave Athens after the record was finished. He was standing at my door, rain pouring down outside on a typical southern January winter's day. He was holding his briefcase in his hand, ready to head out to the airport. [And] Dan Russell (VOL's manager) had called, [and] had just told us that Vigilantes of Love had been accepted to play the coveted New Band Showcase at the 1992 Cornerstone Festival, a Christian festival south of Chicago. We (the band) were pretty green and uninformed about the CCM thing, and what we knew about it we thought was pretty cheesy. I knew Mark had made a living playing to it, so to speak, and then subsequently outgrown it artistically, and now seemed to have no place to fall, professionally speaking. Anyway, I remember expressing my deeper reservations about VOL participating in the festival, since we really were a band without an agenda, religious or otherwise. (Sure, we dealt with some of the big themes in music like sin, loss, brokenness and redemption; but we did so in non-preachy ways and from a very privatized perspective; we just wanted our music taken at face value.) I wanted VOL to continue to play in clubs and college bars which is where we came out of, so I asked him if he thought doing that festival was a good idea, or might it possibly tag us as a Christian band?

Mark's reply was pretty cryptic, [but] he made it clear he was referring to ALL CCM type shows: "Stay as far away from that as you possibly can," was his short reply, and then he left. I never saw him face to face again, but I'll never forget the moment. It's all still very fresh 10 years later. I can still hear his voice; see him in that long black coat he wore, looking at the floor, as he answered my question in his soft voice. In Mark's mind it was all pretty clear at that point: On one side of the fence it was either music about honesty, integrity, credibility and passion OR, on the other side, the musically trivializing and dumbing down of the Gospel of Christ (but all for a good paycheck!). Even now sometimes I berate myself for trying to straddle that fence.

That Mark's talent was recognizable by someone as (commercially) successful in the mainstream market as Peter Buck—though it was, as Bill said, an encouraging validation—must have added to Mark's frustration at feeling trapped in the subculture. You can understand, therefore, the deep feelings behind the advice he gave to Bill, whom Mark had referred to as the most talented songwriter he had ever worked with. In fact, John Austin related to me that Mark had given similar advice to Sam Phillips. When she got her first record contract offer, it was from a Christian label, and Mark told her that she ought to think hard about it because they were going to try and turn her into some blonde Christian singer. There is a certain irony that must be noted in the fact that Mark himself, along with Bill, accepted an invitation to play the Cornerstone festival that year.

With respect to that pressure to be simple as a producer as well as songwriter, the famous "Play it Stupider" sessions have reached the status of legend among Mark's fans and friends. (See "The Radio-April 1990" p.200) Chris Hauser was one of the promotions people for Myrrh Records involved in this project on the "other side"—that is, as one of the "industry folks" who worked on radio airplay. Chris readily admitted to Mark what he called the sad truth. "I told [Mark and Tom Willett] that, sad but true, radio was appealing (and I suppose always has and always will be) to a lowest common denominator [with respect to both] sound and lyric content." In other words, Mark was not exaggerating the situation. Chris specifically told them, "if they could come up with a ballad that drew parallels between a natural every day experience and the eternal, [then] Christian radio would eat it up." As a huge fan of Mark's, and one fully aware of Mark's genius, Chris was embarrassed to have to tell them that. Yet he knew it was true.

What Mark's version of the story may underplay, however, is how much Mark actually wanted to attain that "radio success" for the album. According to Chris, it was Mark and Tom who approached him "to find out exactly what kind of songs Christian radio stations were playing at the time and how they could get another hit for" the artist involved. And, in fact, they did succeed: the song peaked at #2 on the contemporary christian radio charts. As Chris described, the lyric:

> . . . was absolutely a lowest common denominator type song and it turns out Mark was the writer but was so embarrassed by the lyric they listed this songwriter as an Italian version of his real name: *Giovanni* (Italian for John) *Audiori* (past tense of the verb "to hear").

Of course it would itself be a gross over-simplification to say that Mark's frustrations with the christian music industry were based only—or even primarily—on the issues of musical and lyrical shallowness, or on the pressures to adhere to (or imitate) that triviality. As Mark chronicled in his own diary, and as we will explore later in this book, he also had theological frustrations with what he felt to be a gnostic anti-artistic influence in the church.

Pat Terry and Chuck Long both also felt like Mark was in some way reacting against aspects of what they described as "Southern Christianity." Pat commented:

> Flannery O'Connor said the South was "Christ-haunted." As a Southerner I understand that. There is something about a version of Christianity that is very common in the South. You find it in Baptist churches, Methodist churches, and Presbyterian churches. There are different versions of it because of the subtle and not-so-subtle [denominational] differences in theology but it's all basically the same: there's tons of guilt! *Tons* of guilt. And it's all risen up to an image of what your church community expects you to be. And Mark, because he came into the world as

such an individual, it was very hard on him being a Southerner in a lot of ways.

I think what probably helped him come alive creatively was when he moved to California. There was less of that feeling of being under scrutiny.

Chuck described it as an imperative to fit a particular pattern, and a sense that somebody was always watching over you. "[Mark] actually loved the South—everything that made up the richness of the South . . . He loved the mountains. He was very clued into his environment wherever he was," Chuck explained. "[And] he got along great with his dad and loved his dad." There was also a very rich story-telling tradition in the South, and in the Southern characters surrounding Mark, whose wonderful influence on Mark's songwriting cannot be overlooked. And yet the South also drove him crazy in other ways, as Chuck noted more than once in our conversation. "I think I've known a lot of expatriate Southerners; they love the South but they don't want to live in the South." With respect to Mark in particular, Chuck explained, "I think there was anxiousness and a pervasive guilty feeling, but you're not really sure [about what]. It was in the air. [Mark] couldn't stand to be [in the South] for more than a few days at a time.

It was more than this that Mark reacted against, however. In his adult life, he had also been hurt deeply and on numerous occasions by people within the world of christendom (and not just its Southern manifestations): from producers to concert promoters to pastors.[13] And yet, acknowledging the many contributing factors, the focal point (or at least the starting point) in Mark's reaction against this industry was his aversion to over-simplification of both musical and lyrical elements: a choice that Mark eventually came to see as being between "honesty, integrity, credibility and passion" set against "the musically trivializing and dumbing down of the Gospel of Christ."

IS IT ANY WONDER?

In any case, *Mosaics* was Mark's last album of original material released by Home Sweet Home. It was at the end of this period that WHAT? Records began to be formed. Getting an exact history of this endeavor is not easy as there were many people involved, they were coming from many different places, and the project kept shifting shapes. The initial vision for the label came from a group of artists including Mark Heard, T-Bone Burnett, and

Tonio K. Several other songwriters and musicians also got involved at various times (David Edwards, Paul Potash, Randy Stonehill, etc.), along with one non-musician, Tim Alderson, who happened to be good friends with several of the musicians.

As Tonio K. described it, he, T-Bone, and Mark had this great idea for coming up with an album. They would each contribute about three songs, maybe co-write a song or two, and then just shop that album around until somebody bought it. But the vision changed as different people got involved. Before long, talk began to move to the idea of the artists recording and marketing their own album—essentially founding their own label, though at the time independent labels had not yet hit the scene. Tim Alderson expanded on this story:

> We decided what we were going to do. Everybody was out of a record deal. Nobody had a deal and everybody had a backlog of songs, and everybody was unhappy . . . So we talked about how we were going to make this record and we had this whole scheme.
>
> [The question arose] "Who's going to do it? Who's actually going to take responsibility?" and T-Bone pointed to me and said, "You. You'll do it!"
>
> So we had this idea, this very clever idea—and you know it might have worked now because of the electronic media, [but] in those days you had to press albums and there was money involved—we had this scheme that everyone in the room was going to contribute a song. And we'd end up with twelve cuts. Some guys already had masters that they owned . . . and the ones who didn't Mark would record. And so everybody started bringing tapes in or we'd pass around the guitar . . . and everyone would listen. Like thirty producers and one artist.

Of course with the incredible talent assembled in that room, coming up with enough songs was never the problem. It was finding a way to pay for the recording—that is, a way to sell the albums—that was the issue. But they had a plan for that, too, Tim explains:

> Everybody was pumped up, ready to go. The theory was that we were going to record this thing, because we could get the masters done at no cost because people either had masters or

could record them [with Mark]. I could do all the packaging and artwork and stuff. And we had the thing like all ready to go . . . All these guys had some kind of mailing list. So the idea was we would put out a newsletter that would go out—we would pool the mailing list . . . everybody would contribute articles, ideas, and this and that, creative writings, whatever. In the newsletter we would announce the compilation. And then we'd start accepting orders with payment. We'd presell. Mail order laws said you have a certain amount of time to deliver a product or return the check. So we figured we'd start collecting money. If we get enough in time to press the thing and ship it, we do that. If we don't, we'll send the checks back.

Part of the irony of the situation was that while most of the artists in the room had been recording for christian labels, and were frustrated and trying to escape because they weren't being allowed the artistic freedom to grow within that subculture, at least one artist had been recording for mainstream labels and was equally frustrated because he felt like his freedom to express aspects of his faith were being also being suppressed; he had one song called "Too Cool to be a Christian" which he was sure the christian labels would love because Capitol wouldn't record it.

Whatever the goals and causes of frustration, the project was doomed to failure. As Tim concluded, they were greatly lacking in realism about what the real problems were:

There's an oxymoron in the [phrase] "Music Business." Musicians do not understand the business side of the business, and business guys do not understand [the music]. Both sides just don't get the other side. And it's this unholy marriage that just has to exist and it's always a problem . . . I was the only non-musician there and I was the only music-business type, and I didn't know the music business from my butt . . .

So it was a great idea. The only problem was we were working with a roomful of musicians. And there's like this genetic disorder that's involved in being a musician that requires one to be an absolute, complete flake. And they all were. And they were looking at me like I'm supposed to do everything. [But the moment] I start to bring up some practical issues, oh man was that unpopular! . . . I started talking about the nuts and bolts of getting this stuff pressed, it was like fingers in the air . . . They just didn't want to hear it.

Though the vision of that collection of artists never materialized quite as they imagined, two things did come of those meetings. One was that Mark actually began a newsletter, called the *Fingerprint Communiqué*—the only one of the group of artists to follow through on that idea.

The second development was more significant. Somewhere along the line, Tom Willett, who was then working with Word Records, got wind of the plans and got excited by the possibilities. Initially Tom merely offered to help with duplication and mailings of newsletters from out of his Word Records office, but the whole newsletter project got stalled, as most of the artists never actually produced anything for it. So then Tom started talking about making the project into a real label that Word might help distribute. And then discussion moved toward Word co-owning the label, and eventually evolved to Word owning the label outright but the musicians managing it.

Thus came the birth of WHAT? Records, which would be co-distributed: to the contemporary christian music market through Word Records, and to the mainstream market through A&M. By the time the label got off the ground, however, most of the artists had found other venues for their work. Of that group, only Tonio K., Mark Heard, and Dave Perkins would record albums with WHAT? Tonio released two: *Romeo Unchained*, and *Notes from the Lost Civilization*. Interestingly enough, the second of those two was released in two versions, with the Word version removing the song "What Women Want" (which used the word "sex").

Mark Heard released only one album, *Tribal Opera*, through WHAT? Records. If *Mosaics* was seen as a musical departure from his earlier material, *Tribal Opera* was like an entirely different art form—though the lyrics remained as insightful and poetic as ever. In fact, the album was not released as a "Mark Heard album" at all. In an effort to break free from all expectations, Mark created a band image called iDEoLA and released the album under that name. However a close look at the credits revealed that in fact Mark wrote all the songs, and played essentially all of the instruments. The single "Is it Any Wonder" got about one week of airplay on MTV, which was then still in its heyday.

DARLING WHEN I WAS YOUR AGE

Unfortunately WHAT? Records was a short-lived label. The years that followed—with the failure of WHAT? Records and the iDEoLA project—became even more difficult and discouraging for Mark Heard. For a time, Mark seemed to have given up altogether on making records. Through all the discouragement, however, something of his sentimental side remained a part of his character, and it resurfaced in a new and surprising way before his life ended.

On February 18, 1988, Janet gave birth to daughter Rebecca, and Mark became a father for the first time. His sister Susan remembers the phone call she received from the proud new father. "Mark called to tell me it was a girl and said 'I already love her!' I think he was astonished that he could feel this so immediately." Indeed, there was a sudden peace and contentment in his life: a peace that seemed to put some of his other troubles in perspective. Mark's friend Joel Russell saw this. "Mark turned a corner around Rebecca's birth. There was peace in his life that hadn't been there before." Mark would be out in his studio engineering an album—maybe frustrated or having a difficult time—and Rebecca would show up at the door, and Mark's eyes would just light up. Or he'd be working on a new instrument that he didn't know really well, and it wouldn't be working out, and he'd go outside and see Rebecca, and he'd just embrace her and it would be the biggest relief, and suddenly he'd be completely happy again.

"There was definitely a change," Chuck Long agrees. "When you saw Mark with his daughter, there was a caring fatherliness there that I had never seen before in him."

Pat Terry still has a recording of the phone call he received after Mark became a father:

> When Rebecca was born, he called me. I still have the answering machine tape. You could hear the transformation in his voice. He said something to the effect of, "She is quite beautiful." You could really hear how thrilled he was. I think that was a huge thing.

Mark's good friend Julie Miller saw the same thing. "He was mystified and enamored with Rebecca," she recalls.[14] She tells how Mark would often come over to visit her, bringing Rebecca in tow, and when he didn't have her with him, then he'd be full of stories *about* her.

An irony of this is that, from several accounts, Mark didn't really want children. Phil Madeira recalls a scene from their early friendship.

> The first time my wife Elinor and I met Mark and Janet, we hit it off. We wound up driving around New England with them, from Maine to Boston. I remember in the course of getting to know them, naively asking "do you plan on having kids?"
>
> Suffice to say that this is a question one ceases to ask as one matures! But it was out there, and Mark hit the roof. He went on and on saying, "I HATE kids," all the while Janet quietly watching by. Well, having kids IS pretty scary, and I guess his remark probably hearkened to that fear more than it did reflect genuine loathing. Obviously, by the time he and Janet had a child, those were words which had long been swallowed.

Whatever words Mark used in the heat of that moment, there are many indications that the reality of his feelings was somewhat different from what he was willing to express aloud. Certainly he was hesitant to have children, but despite his occasional protestations to the contrary, that hesitancy seems not to have come from any dislike of children. Chuck recounts:

> He was around my kids, and was very pleasant with my daughter when he would come see us. He was not the "Get the kids out of here!" kind of guy at all. He was never like that. I had other friends that were like that.
>
> I think in some ways Sandra and I having kids before he did, he was curious about it. Nothing went by him. He didn't miss anything when he was around you.

Rather, Mark's reluctance to have kids seemed to come largely from his fears: fears that he might not express in conversation with even an intimate friend, but which for a songwriter will inevitably surface in his music—in songs like "Satellite Sky," "Why, Mama, Why?" "Worry Too Much," "Another Good Lie," or "Broken Man."

Fear of what? Fear of the unknown perhaps. Of the world his child would grow up in.

> I want to laugh for my children
>
> I want the spark to ignite
>
> Before they find out what it's like

To be born into these times

> —"Why, Mama, Why?"

It's the children of my children

It's these lambs born in innocence

It's wondering if the good I've known

Will last to be seen by the eyes of the little ones

> —"Worry Too Much"

Sometimes it feels like bars of steel I cannot bend

  with my hands

Oh Oh I worry too much.

> —"Worry Too Much"

Or perhaps simply fear of his own inadequacy to be a good father.

It can't be easy for my children

I'm hollow before my time.

> —"Why, Mama, Why?"

I have faltered in my youth

I have wanted to do everything right

> —"Broken Man"

Pat Terry reflected on this:

The period before he became a father he had his concerns about having children. I mean he couldn't imagine it. I always interpreted some of that as his feelings of inadequacy—like "I don't know what kind of a father I can be." I mean, he felt like he had his hands full enough just being Mark Heard and doing what he did . . .

He saw everything. The longer he lived, the longer he looked at the world. When he thought about having kids, he thought "Oh, they're coming into *this* world."

In hindsight, Mark's fears came out in other ways also—ways seemingly unrelated to having children. Joel Russell recalls when he and his wife Rebecca were first married. Mark knew that Joel was from a big family, and wanted to know if he was planning on having kids of his own, and if so how he would manage it. "I just don't know how you deal with it," Mark would say. "How's it going to be in this age? It's just going to be really tough."

And it was tough, both for parent and child. Speaking again of the change in Mark, Chuck went on, "It was a profound change—there was no doubt about it—and definitely for the better. But, I think, along with that came a worry that he hadn't had before." As Pat Terry put it, "I think the world looked a little scarier after that . . . because there was something he cared about that was innocent and good."

It is something of that innocence—and Mark's sense of it—that we catch a glimpse of in the song "Another Good Lie." Written from the perspective of a parent to a child ("Darling when I was your age . . . "), the song carries a warning of the pains that are to come from living in a fallen world, especially the pain of being hurt by others: "And baby then they took my heart / And vanished like a memory / Leaving it to time and circumstance / To come deliver me." Certainly Mark's fears about raising children did not cease after his child was born, but grew even more pointed in the context of his deep love for his own daughter. Perhaps the most poignant line in this song, however, is the start of the bridge: "Baby I'm just one man / And my world fell apart long ago."

Looking back many years later, Phil Madeira gained a new perspective on the whole interaction he'd had with Mark over the topic of children, as he put Mark's fears of having children in context with many other fears.

> Of course, Rebecca's birth changed all that. In retrospect, I think that episode revealed a lot of Mark's fears that seemed to have a lot to do with things he couldn't control—air travel, kids, life.

> Of course, that is just one moment sandwiched between many others of hilarity and sweetness within a few days. We laughed a lot on our little road trip. The only other incident was that our little Volkswagen Dasher lost its brakes on our way to Logan Airport in Boston. I didn't say much, but once we were in the Callahan Tunnel, which goes under the Mystic River (I think), Mark realized that I was using the handbrake [because my other brake was broken]. He was already nervous about having to fly, and here he was careening along with no brakes in the middle of

Boston's nightmare traffic!

Even Janet did not come fully to understand this aspect of Mark's insecurities until nearly a decade after he died. "Mark was very excited when Rebecca was born," she agreed, yet she realized that there was something else at work in Mark's heart that was much deeper than his visible excitement at the time. More than nine years after Mark's death, Janet found a journal that he had written for their young Rebecca. "In it he said that he prayed a prayer to God and asked that she be brought into our lives as He saw fit. He told her in the journal that he [had] never told me [about this prayer] and it's true, he didn't. So he was thinking about it more than I realized. I just think he was nervous about being a good father."

And so Rebecca truly was an answer to prayer, and she became a gift to Mark in more ways than one. Not only did she bring him joy, but as Joel Russell describes she brought him a deeper sense of his own humanity and need for God. "The way Rebecca filled Mark's life, I think, was so opposite in that it helped complete more of who he was and broadened his lyrics. I think it also made things sharper and harder in the grand world where, 'Now, gosh, I have a child to care for.'"

"I remember Rebecca inviting me on more than one occasion to join her in coloring the sidewalks with colored chalks," recalls John Austin of the time he spent recording his first record with Mark. "I could tell it pained Mark to have to tell her the sobering reality of 'No . . . No, I'm sorry honey we will have to do that later. John and I have to go to work now.'" One of my own last memories of a conversation with Mark was listening to him tell me how he was looking forward to taking Rebecca to the zoo soon.

In the end, I think the clearest understanding, both of how Mark felt before Rebecca was born and also of how he changed after she came along, are best and most simply expressed in Mark's own words in the journal he wrote to her[15]:

> I had not spent much time with children; what time I had spent was not perceived by me as pleasant. Other parents told me when they are your own, you'll feel differently. I found out later that I did—it was not hard to be around you or to love you, at all.

ANOTHER GOOD LIE

1991, *Second Hand*

Darling when I was your age

I could do anything

There were days of rock 'n roll

And lunar strolls and friendship rings

And baby I told myself

I'd follow my deepest dreams

Knowing if I did my best

Success would always follow me

It was another good lie

Coming down like a freezing rain

From a hot blue sky

Another good lie

Coming in like a crosstown

Hurricane on fire

Another good lie

Coming down on your Daddy's soul

Til it made him old

Another good lie

Another good lie

Another good lie

Darling they all told me

That they would do anything

Climb the highest mountain

Swim the ocean

Do the damnedest things
And baby then they took my heart
And vanished like a memory
Leaving it to time and circumstance
To come deliver me

It was another good lie
Coming down like a freezing rain
From a hot blue sky
Another good lie
Coming in like a crosstown
Hurricane on fire
Another good lie
Coming down on your Daddy's soul
Til it made him old
Another good lie
Another good lie
Another good lie

Baby I'm just one man
And my world fell apart long ago
I guess I'm still in shock
It shouldn't have been like that
I guess I still hope for deliverance

Darling when I was your age
I could do anything
I could be a restless heart

A social force

Or just genuine

And baby don't our dreams die hard

In the ashes of destiny

I wish that I could lay to rest

The bitterness that keeps telling me

About another good lie

Coming down like a freezing rain

From a hot blue sky

Another good lie

Coming in like a crosstown

Hurricane on fire

Another good lie

Coming down on your Daddy's soul

Til it made him old

Another good lie

Another good lie

Another good lie

YOUR WORLD OR MINE

1987, previously unreleased

One of us will never grow up

Hanging on to fantasy

The other one grins and bears it

Saying, "God bless reality"

Talking like total strangers

On the tower of Babel

Your world or mine tonight

Your world or mine all of the time

Your world or mine tonight

Your world and mine collide

One of us is palms and tropics

Want to make a Winter warm

The other one's poems and topics

Want to thaw a chilly heart

Drifters from different seas

A pair of refugees

Your world or mine tonight

Your world or mine all of the time

Your world or mine tonight

Your world and mine collide

One of us is trying so hard

To be a better human being

While the other one grins and bears it

Saying, "Love is what you need!"
We're aliens from outer space
With smiles on our faces

Your world or mine tonight
Your world or mine all of the time
Your world or mine tonight
Your world and mine collide

HOLD ME CLOSER
1989, previously unreleased

We could be a little colder

With the cunning of our kind

We can be as mediocre

As the heros of our time

Imagine your supply of love depends on your demand

Funny how the look of love depends on where you stand

HOLD ME CLOSER

CLOSER THAN A CLOSEST FRIEND

HOLD ME CLOSER

DISREGARD THE VIOLINS

HOLD ME CLOSER

CLOSER THAN AN AUGUST NIGHT

CLOSER THAN CLOSE

IN A FIGHT THAT ONLY TWO CAN WIN

We could be a little better

Or we might get a little worse

We could write ourselves a letter

About the choice that we prefer

Funny how reality depends on how you feel

Or maybe our emotions tend to lean on what is real

HOLD ME CLOSER

CLOSER THAN A CLOSEST FRIEND

HOLD ME CLOSER

DISREGARD THE VIOLINS

HOLD ME CLOSER

CLOSER THAN AN AUGUST NIGHT

CLOSER THAN CLOSE

IN A FIGHT THAT ONLY TWO CAN WIN

It could be our salvation

Or maybe it's our curse

The chronic resurrection

Of the crimes we wanna purge

Either way there ain't no point in digging up them bones

We've got the night all to ourselves and nights don't last too long

HOLD ME CLOSER

CLOSER THAN A CLOSEST FRIEND {Siamese twin}

HOLD ME CLOSER

DISREGARD THE VIOLINS

HOLD ME CLOSER

CLOSER THAN AN AUGUST NIGHT

CLOSER THAN CLOSE

IN A FIGHT THAT ONLY TWO CAN WIN

NOBODY AT ALL
1987, previously unreleased

Shoot me with love and I'll die

But a pistol of blanks points at my eyes

It is no wonder that I blunder into worlds that you can't understand

Walk with me in the rain

Don't ask me why

And if there's no room for thunder in your blue sky

I have no secrets

But I'll keep things to myself if you can't help me cry

Nobody at all—that's who I can trust besides you

Nobody at all—that's who I can talk to

Nobody at all—that's who I would be without you

Nobody at all—that's who could replace you

Take me out on the floor in the crowd

Would you rather just talk and sit this one out

What kind of dancer am I

Asking all these questions to myself out loud

  CHORUS

Look at us both and it's true

All the classical symptoms of two fools

Who would suggest

That circumstance could keep romance from taking me and you

SUDDEN STRANGER

1987, previously unreleased

We've not agreed to disagree
How come this sudden catastrophe
Are we to be or not to be
Give me some predictability

Sudden stranger will you break my heart
Sudden stranger do I know you
Charming changer I don't want no war
Sudden stranger

If you betray me I'll play dumb
Where are these tendencies coming from
Will you repay me eye for eye
For all the lies that I've tried to hide

If love is a word you can't pronounce
What do you think-it's the thought that counts
If you should need me here I am
I know you'll make me whole given half a chance

[Mark Heard, Switzerland]

{4}

ORPHANS OF GOD

"I've been writing the same song for

twenty-five years. They're all the same. Yeah, you

just listen to all my songs. They're just the same songs

written over and over in different ways."

—Mark Heard

ORPHANS OF GOD

1992, *Satellite Sky*

I will rise from my bed with a question again
As I work to inherit the restless wind
The view from my window is cold and obscene
I want to touch what my eyes haven't seen
But they have packaged our virtue in cellulose dreams
And sold us the remnants 'til our pockets are clean
'Til our hopes fall 'round our feet like the dust of dead leaves
and we end up looking like what we believe
We are soot-covered urchins running wild and unshod
We will always be remembered as the orphans of God
They will dig up these ruins and make flutes of our bones
and blow a hymn to the memory of the orphans of God

Like bees in a bottle we are flying at fate
Beating our wings against the walls of this place
Unaware that the struggle is the blood of the proof
In choosing to believe the unbelievable truth
But they have captured our siblings and rendered them mute
They've disputed our lineage and poisoned our roots
We have bought from the brokers who have broken their oaths
And we're out on the streets with a lump in our throats
We are soot-covered urchins running wild and unshod
We will always be remembered as the orphans of God
They will dig up these ruins and make flutes of our bones
and blow a hymn to the memory of the orphans of God

WITH A QUESTION AGAIN

In the previous chapter, we touched both on the end of Mark Heard's relationship with Home Sweet Home Records, and also on the brief life of iDEoLA and WHAT? Records. Both of these episodes, which took place back-to-back in the mid-1980s, left him frustrated and discouraged. If we step back and look again where Mark was a decade earlier, we might gain a better understanding of some of the influences that helped shape his thinking, and perhaps better see why he responded as he did to certain situations, ideas, and pressures. In particular, this period of Mark's life—the period following his graduation from college—was framed by two key sets of events (his time at L'Abri and his move to Los Angeles), two important developing friendships (Chuck Long and Pat Terry), and his first two jobs out of college (teaching Bible at a Christian School and working in a chicken-feeder factory).

As mentioned earlier, one of Mark's oldest friends was Chuck Long, and many stories about Mark keep coming back to him, including the trip to L'Abri that they took together in 1975, and for which Chuck was a big part of the impetus. Chuck and Mark met largely because they both lived in the same town, Macon, and their families went to the same church. Around 1973, while Mark was still in college, their mothers were talking with each other and decided that their sons should get together (since they both liked music). So Jean Heard essentially *made* her son Mark go over to Chuck's house. "And if you knew Mark," Chuck relates, "you knew that making [him] do something wasn't easy to do, and his attitude was not going to be good if you made him do something he didn't want to do." So, while Mark consented to his mother's wishes and visited Chuck, it was not with a particularly positive mindset. "We played guitar a little bit," Chuck continues the story, "and he was clearly much better at guitar than I was. We enjoyed being around each other, and he relaxed after he got over the fact that his mother made him do it." In fact, they soon became close friends.

Mark graduated from the University of Georgia the next year, in 1974. His first job out of college was teaching a theology and Bible class at the First Presbyterian Day School. Mark and Chuck moved from close friends to inseparable friends. As Chuck recalls:

> That [next] year I was home working steel construction and
> Mark was teaching school and we spent pretty much every

afternoon together for that whole fall. We were sort of thrown together, and everybody was off to college, and he was home from college because he had finished, and I wasn't sure what I was doing at that point. We spent pretty much every day together. Mark was writing a lot of stuff, and he wrote the [material] that became *On Turning to Dust* [his first solo album].

In the winter quarter of 1975, however, Chuck headed off to the University of Georgia up in Athens, while Mark stayed home in Macon and taught the rest of the year. "He would come up every weekend just 'cause there was nobody at home to hang out with. He was playing and recording a lot, I guess, but he didn't have many kindred spirits in Macon at that time."

It was around then that the idea of going to study at L'Abri came up. L'Abri was a study center conceived, begun, and run by Francis and Edith Schaeffer: a place where people could go and study, under the Schaeffer's tutelage, any of a broad range of topics dealing with Christianity and culture. In particular, it was meant to be a place where people were free to ask questions and express doubts, as long as they were willing to look for answers. Yet it was more than just a place to study; it was a *community* where the students also took part in the day-to-day life including gardening, cleaning, cooking, and all the chores necessary to keep the place running. L'Abri had originally started in Switzerland, but later expanded with the opening of several other L'Abri centers around the world including one across the border in France.

As a student at the University of Georgia, Mark had been involved with Campus Crusade for Christ. He had even gone on a summer project with them to Ithaca, New York (where he met his future wife Janet). But in the winter of 1975, he was asking lots of questions about faith and art. It was around that time that Dr. Francis Schaeffer came to First Presbyterian Church in Macon. Both Chuck and Mark had read some of his books, which weren't broadly read at that time (though they have since come to be much more widely read).[16] In particular, Dr Schaeffer, though evangelical in his faith, was not seen as mainstream evangelical, largely because his approach was pretty different. "He was a powerful speaker," Chuck recalls, "and held in high regard by a lot of people. He was a very grace-filled individual. His way of dealing with people and speaking with people was very impressive, and Mark felt that way too."

Dr. Schaeffer was also just what Mark needed: somebody who took seriously not only the Christian faith, but also the value of art, and the importance of understanding the culture we live in and how to communicate within that culture. He also understood the importance of asking questions, and of allowing questions. Chuck concludes the story:

[Mark] was going through a lot of [wondering] where his faith fit in with his music, and how that was going to work. Because at this point, I think, the Campus Crusade ministry approach was not where he was headed and he had figured that out by that time. And that fall he was pretty pensive . . .

I was really just getting to know him at that time. I knew Mark was an amazing guitar-player and songwriter, and a great singer, and I admired him for all that, and loved his music. But I didn't appreciate at that point how profound a thinker he was, although I studied philosophy in college and we talked about a lot of stuff that fall and winter and spring . . .

[Anyway] I had always wanted to go to L'Abri, and my parents, who were overseas at the time, had agreed to send me. If I could arrange it, they would pay. And Mark had always wanted to go.

So after hearing Dr. Schaeffer speak, the two decided to try to go. They contacted L'Abri, and were told that there were positions open in the summer of 1975. After a couple weeks of traveling around Europe in June—including a hilarious two-day stop in Iceland, and then two nights sleeping in a pig barn waiting for their L'Abri room to open up—they spent a month and a half studying at French L'Abri. Two days a week they would head over to Swiss L'Abri: one day a week for worship, and one day a week for study and to hear Francis Schaeffer lecture. "For me it was just a great time of being in Europe," Chuck reflects back. "I enjoyed being there, but I wasn't that serious of a student. Mark was a much more serious student. He went there with a lot more in his mind."

Though Mark's initial time at L'Abri preceded his marriage, Janet was still aware of the impact that time had on her husband's life:

I think the biggest impact L'Abri had for Mark was to have a place where he could ask questions and not be dismissed. Music [and] art was not considered a waste of one's time; in other words, it has value. It was a well-rounded experience too. There was time for study, but you also had to work in the garden or cook or clean.

Janet also described one of Mark's later meetings with Dr. Schaeffer, when she and Mark returned to Switzerland together:

> Mark talked with him about being a musician and how much he loved it and could he be sure that this was what God wanted him to do. Mark struggled with this for a long time. Dr. Schaeffer was encouraging. Christians in the arts do have a valid place in the world. Mark had so much respect for Dr. Schaeffer. To hear this from him meant a lot.

Given Chuck and Janet's observations, it is not surprising that the influence of Francis Schaeffer's writing can be seen in several of Mark's albums especially his idea of presuppositional apologetics (explored in *The God Who Is There* [1968]). The song "Orphans of God" (as discussed later in this chapter) explores the outcome of accepting the post-Nietzschean proposition of God's death, while the entire album *Mosaics* (also discussed later in this chapter) deals fundamentally with our humanness in a way reflective of Schaeffer's *Back to Freedom and Dignity* [1972]—which itself addresses materialist and Darwinian presuppositions by way of a response to B. F. Skinner's *Beyond Freedom and Dignity* [1971].[17]

Not surprisingly, Mark returned to visit L'Abri several more times over the next few years, including at least three trips with Janet. He loved to perform for Swiss audiences. "Christians and non-Christians would attend the concerts and were so open to listening to what was being said through the songs," Janet explained. "The venues were so varied too, from small halls to beautiful old churches, to rooms in castles."

Mark particularly hit it off well with one of the Schaeffer's daughters, Prisca Sandri, and with their son-in-law, John Sandri. Both Prisca and John were very interested in music and art. Prisca would often play Mark's music and have discussions with people who were studying at L'Abri. Mark's friendship with her lasted the rest of his life.

Another of Mark's friendships that lasted the next two decades was with Pat Terry. Pat was getting to know Mark about the same time Chuck was. In fact, neither of them is sure who met Mark first. Pat and Mark initially connected because both were performing at the same banquet event. Pat was already well on his way to an established career in music within the contemporary christian music scene. (His band, The Pat Terry Group, would record several successful albums in the mid-1970s.) At the time, Mark was connected with a band called Infinity Plus Three. Pat was really impressed because, although the band was "just a bunch of college kids," Mark was performing original songs. Pat's sense was that Mark was the only one in the band—or maybe one of two—who seemed like a real musician. They met and hit it off.

> I used to go visit Mark. He lived in an apartment off campus. I used to go there and stay. He had a couple of two-track recorders and we would record things in his little apartment. We'd bounce tracks back and forth on these things so we'd end up with a multi-track thing. And Mark had tons of stuff like that that he already had.

> I particularly remember going up and staying and rehearsing with him. We did a concert together along with another friend, Ron Moore, out on the Quadrangle. It was sponsored by Campus Crusade for Christ. Mark was real involved with that at the time.

This friendship, like his friendship with Chuck, took off. Pat recalls a time more than a year after Mark's graduation. Mark had left Macon and his job teaching at the day school, and moved to Smyrna, Georgia where he worked at a factory that built machinery used to feed chickens. He was living there in a little cabin, which he shared with one other person. As Pat Terry recalls:

> It was pretty rough . . . He was working at the Spinks Chicken Feeder factory, and he wasn't making much money. He was barely getting by and was depressed about the work he was doing at the factory. He wanted to be doing music. I'd go visit him at night, and we'd play guitars, and he would heat apple vinegar on the stove and we'd drink it straight. It tasted pretty terrible, but Mark had this theory about its medicinal values, which was really his way of selling me on the concept of drinking it. I think he had some idea that it was a cool, bohemian thing to do. It was funny really. He was living on hamburgers from Burger King . . . that kind of thing. I'd ask, "Have you eaten yet?" and he'd say "No," and I'd say "Let's fix something here." But there was nothing in the house. I mean, *nothing*. You'd be lucky to find even soup and crackers. He was basically still living like a college student. But regardless of the circumstances, I think he enjoyed the independence. He was

feeling his way around, looking for a future.

Although this period of Mark's life did not last too long, Mark makes occasional reference to it in his journals: "I have worked in a factory, and one becomes a bit hypnotized after some time to the point where all one can think about is going home, watching TV, having a beer and going to bed." [From "Confessional" p.194] Memories of being hungry and poor may also have had significant influence on Mark in his later life, evident in his concern over providing for his family in a way that would not put them in a situation like he had been in during his chicken-feeder-factory days.

Even during this time, however, Mark's creative side was constantly at work, and his humor remained constant. Pat Terry concludes:

> My memory of that time was just how much Mark's sense of humor [stayed with him]—those nights were spent making nonsense songs. I do remember during that period that Mark was really anxious to be doing music. He was working because it was his only opportunity he had at the time to make a living, but where his heart was, was to do music.

ASPHALT OCEAN ROARS

As mentioned earlier in the book, Mark Heard and Janet Currin married on April 2, of 1977. In November of that year, they moved to Los Angeles. Perhaps it had to do with his new life in the big city, or perhaps it had more to do with his experience at L'Abri, or maybe it was a combination of both. Whatever the case, although Mark always retained something of the shy Georgia-boy in him, when he and Janet made their permanent move to California certain aspects of his outlook on life began to change.

One of Mark's first new friends when he moved to Los Angeles was fellow songwriter Tom Howard. Tom still remembers those early days of their friendship. Though Mark "was a thoughtful person from the get-go," he became even more so. "The Mark Heard he became—the Mark Heard of 1992—[was] very thoughtful." As Tom described:

> What strikes me profoundly is the cultural shift that took place in Mark's life from the time I first met him when he came up from Georgia . . .
>
> I was quite involved with the making of *Victims of the Age*. That was probably my closest association with Mark. I mean I had a lot

of involvement with *Appalachian Melody*, but there we were just getting to know each other. With *Victims of the Age*, he had turned some kind of sociological-culture corner, which is obvious in the lyrical content, and in the musical elements.

[What brought that about?] I think exposure to Los Angeles to begin with. I think a total reevaluation of his roots. Not so much the Southernness of it, but the closed-mindedness of it, and the rather Calvinistic enclosure that he finds himself in, particularly at school and so forth.

This cultural awareness and growing social consciousness—particularly with respect to the harsh realities of city-life—was evident in many of the songs such as "Victims of the Age," "City Life," or the unreleased "Backstreets" which he penned in 1989.

BACKSTREETS

1989, previously unreleased

Beneath the palm trees

See them wave like flags in the warm breeze

They paved up the promised land

And gave us the backstreets

Breathe in the bus fumes

Aphrodisiac—a gift from the tycoons

Who Cadillac through the human boomtown

Here in the backstreets

Ain't no ignorant bliss And no one expects it

This ain't easy street yet   And no one forgets it

LIVING IN THE BACKSTREETS BABY

LIVING IN THE BACKSTREETS GIRL

LIVING IN THE BACKSTREETS BABY

IT'S A BACKSTREET WORLD
LIVING IN THE BACKSTREETS BABY
LIVING IN THE BACKSTREETS NOW
LIVING IN THE BACKSTREETS BABY
LIVING AND LOVING SOMEHOW

Oh the drunks tilt
Down the big boulevards that the banks built
Say your thanks and forget your guilt
Hey this is the backstreets

National fascination
With the footage of the smashing of oppression
Cashing in with a big success
But not in the backstreets

This ain't no limbo of souls, but no one suspects it
This ain't no boulevard of gold, and no one forgets it

CHORUS

Those ivory towers
The ones that point like guns up in downtown
Shoot the stars
And they'll win some wars
But not in the backstreets

Up in the think-tanks
They must be jumping in and drowning like tame rats
Never wondering what's keeping love alive
In the backstreets

Ain't no ignorant bliss and no one expects it

This ain't easy street yet and no one forgets it

CHORUS

In simple terms, we could describe this as a reflection in Mark's music of his profound social concerns, and an awareness of the realities of life in a fallen world. In Mark's case, however, this awareness was more than a distant intellectual observation; it was something he seemed to feel—and to be deeply troubled by—at a very personal level.

Of equal importance, Mark's songwriting soon moved beyond mere observation of the *consequences* of certain societal beliefs and cultural values to a critique of the beliefs and values themselves: a connection between the prevailing worldview that shapes our society and the outcome of accepting such a worldview. In some sense, Mark was exploring through the artistic imagery of song what Francis Schaeffer was writing about more philosophically in his books: a form of presuppositional apologetics. In short, he asked "Why?" *What was the thinking that lay behind what he was seeing?*

In Mark Heard's 1985 release *Mosaics*—which, as documented earlier, had actually been written and recorded before the 1984 release *Ashes and Light*—Mark makes numerous explicit references to our "society," "civilization," "culture," and "age."

> And so we breathe until we die
> The acropolis crumbles
> While humbleness threatens to die
> The culture fiddles while it cries
> The accompaniments to such a sad,
> > self-inflicted demise[18]

> When civilization takes a nasty turn
> And concepts are hushed when books are burned
> All is not lost[19]

> He saw the world through unused eyes

Started ignoring what was cool

And all the lies in society's shrines

Started putting his heart on the line

He rocked the boat and the culture-at-large said,

"We don't want to talk truth or God

Or no other themes of that kind

Or of putting your heart on the line"

So now he blends in with the bourgeoisie

He learned the lesson that society

Rewards only those who decline

To go putting their hearts on the line[20]

They say this is the Golden Age

Video millennium

Tidings from the self-made media sage

Tickings of the bio-bomb[21]

A central theme running through all of *Mosaics* is the importance of being created in God's image: not only the inherent worth of human life ("Life is a miracle/Formed from the chaos/And loved like a blameless child/ . . . We breathe every breath/By the grace of God"), but also the reality and significance of human choice. ("The choices we make will be heard til the end of time."[22]) In particular, the album addresses the popular materialist worldview that man is just a machine and that all our actions are predetermined by genetic, chemical, and biological conditions ("They say this is the Golden Age/In which both virtue and flaw/And the entire human element/Are effects of the quantum laws"[23]).

Through these songs, Mark points out not only that these materialist beliefs[24] are false ("And though molecular/We're so much more than pure machine/Though we forgot our origins."[25]), but that they have disastrous consequences. The album is full of vivid imagery of what happens to a society, civilization, age, or culture which, as a whole, rejects the notions of human worth ("We watch life destroyed as if it were meaningless/Some unborn child (no mother cries)/Some unknown soldier destroyed by lies"[26]), or rejects the belief in human freedom:

> The surface of this sphere
>
> Becomes a playground for the fools
>
> Who twist their words like tools[27]

> Jet-set etiquette consciousness
>
> Monosyllabic goodbyes
>
> No one cares about no one else
>
> We're so used to the capital "I"[28]

In short, Mark saw not only the obvious effects of our cultural values, but he also understood the philosophical presuppositions behind them, and he related the two.

It should not be surprising to find this theme is oft-repeated in Mark's work. Toward the end of Mark's life, Pat Terry was complimenting him on what a great album *Satellite Sky* was—how it was the best thing he'd ever done. Mark replied:

> Well, yeah. I'll be honest with you. I've been writing the same song for twenty-five years. They're all the same. Yeah, you just listen to all my songs. They're just the same songs written over and over in different ways.[29]

Pat thought he understood what Mark was getting at, "that there was a theme there. He knew he hadn't written the same song over. But there's a concept and a point of view, and he's been saying it over and over because that's what he had to say."

This one particular theme—relating worldviews and their consequences—reached its poetic and profound peak in Mark's final three albums. His song "Orphans of God" is one of the most striking examples of this understanding. "I will rise from my bed with a question again," the song begins. That simple line—a longing for truth and answers, or an expression of the pain and confusion engendered by how chaotic the world has become, or perhaps both—could be a defining statement of who Mark was.

A couple lines later the song continues, "I want to touch what my eyes have not seen," expressing a longing that was also evident in a myriad of other Mark Heard songs ("It Will Not Be Like This Forever," "Dry Bones Dance," "Treasure of the Broken Land," etc.): a longing that touches upon the longing for Heaven with imagery that could have come directly from 1 Corinthians 2:9. "No eye has seen, no ear has heard, no mind has conceived what God has prepared for those who love him."

The song continues with references to moral relativism and commercialism—the packaging and selling of virtue—which were two hallmarks of late twentieth-century Western thought. The phrase "inherit the restless wind" may even be a reference to the influence of Darwinism: a subtle twist on the name of the famous play, "Inherit the Wind."

It is the final line of the first verse, however, that captures one of the fundamental realities of this universe: "We end up looking like what we believe." It is what we believe—or Who we believe—that fundamentally determines who we are and how we behave. Tutored as he had been by Francis Schaeffer, Mark understood this all too well. This was precisely the reason that the view from his window was "cold and obscene." In a society that has proclaimed the death of God, we end up looking like orphans. When we dispute our lineage and poison our roots—when we deny our existence as created beings, and devalue humanity—then we end up "out on the streets."

As he wrote in another song on the same album, Mark saw our society not only as lost, but as lost "on purpose." We have become a culture that no longer even *wants* to know the truth. "We could try to figure it out, but the truth might hurt us."

And while "Orphans of God" describes a culture that has proclaimed the death of God and of objective value, the song "Nothing but the Wind" seems to reflect on the resulting hopelessness that is born out of such a culture—the falling of our hope around our feet like the dust of dead leaves:

> If you should see me move toward the light
> You'll shoot me down like a dead satellite
> If you should see me shake on feet of clay
> You'll have me baptized in shades of gray.

When God is proclaimed dead, then we lose our reason for hope. ("If you should see me stoop to smell the rose, don't let me, show me the thorns that it grows.")

HYPOTHETICAL MORTAL BEINGS

So Mark's move to the city, coupled with his time at L'Abri, in some ways helped illuminate more clearly for him the devastating effects of modern and post-modern beliefs, or at least to sharpen and clarify his existing thoughts on those matters. Summarizing that whole transition period, Chuck Long says: "I think that was pretty influential on him. I think he became much more of an expatriate Southerner. He changed a lot during that time—after he moved to L.A. and went to L'Abri a second time . . . He didn't come back home a lot during that period."

It was not only the deceptive worldviews in our society at large that Mark Heard addressed in his songs, however, but the false beliefs that had crept into Christendom. Inside the church, Mark was particularly aware of the effects of modern gnosticism, and various ways it corrupted aspects of church life.

In the liner notes to *Eye of the Storm*, Mark included a personal letter he wrote in which he addressed some of the ways gnosticism had permeated and harmed the Christian church:

> In the gnostic heresy, purity consisted only in the 'spiritual' realm, and had nothing to do with the physical realm. Thought forms paralleling this are present within the church today. The church reacts against 'secular humanism' and in so doing often reacts against humanness. But the two things are not the same at all, and we need to be careful not to throw out the baby with the bath-water. We must stand against humanism, but defend humanness.[30]

Mark went on to describe five areas in which he felt gnosticism had invaded the church. The second of these was one he often addressed in his songwriting.

> Sociological perspective under gnosticism becomes clouded, the positive and the negative aspects of existence losing their polarity in the negation of all human experience, in deference

to the afterlife. Our dignity as created beings is taken from us by such a view, and though it is not often stated in direct form, it is implied and is the logical conclusion of the formative steps of thought borrowed from the school of Plato. Human laughter and human tears are both thought of as inferior to some spiritual pattern for motor response. You might hear, "Don't pay any attention to your hard times—just think about God and you'll forget about them." One reason I wrote "Faces in Cabs," indeed one of the major points of the *Victims Of The Age* album was to reaffirm the reality and value of human life and death, the wonderfulness of the creation of life on earth, and the horribleness of the staining of that wonder by the Fall, and the art of comprehending them simultaneously.[31]

As Mark wrote in this letter, much of the album *Victims of the Age* was in response to gnosticism. Similarly, several songs over a number of albums— "Hold Back Your Tears," "Plastic Halos," "Emotional Man," "We Believe So Well," "I'm In Chains," etc.—affirm the validity of human emotion, especially tears.

Another area where Mark felt a true Christian worldview was being undermined was in the area of creativity. Mark saw the human creative spirit as being fundamental to what it means to be created in God's image.[32] Song-writing, furniture-making, butterfly-collecting, photography, and rug-weaving (to name a number of Mark's own artistic pursuits) are all valuable in and of themselves (for the sake of their beauty), independent of any underlying "message."

While I was in the final stages of work on this book, I was just getting started on a new book[33] on J. R. R. Tolkien's *The Lord of the Rings*. As the writing of these two books overlapped in my thoughts and schedule, I was struck by many similarities between their subjects: Mark Heard and Tolkien—and not merely in the fact that both were brilliant artists and wordsmiths. In both Tolkien and Heard, one can see reflections of a worldview that is firmly anti-gnostic in several ways. In Tolkien, we can see it in the earthiness of his main characters, the hobbits. As evidenced by their abode of choice—hobbit homes are built underground—their values are rooted in the simple pleasures of life: "food and cheer and song."[34] Nowhere is a hobbit happier than sitting around a fire enjoying tea (or beer), cake, a pipe, and conversation with good friends. Rereading some of Mark's criticism of the gnostic influence on the church, it struck me how much he was like a hobbit; as I interviewed many of his friends–Dan Russell, Tom Willett, Chuck Long, Tom Howard, to name a few—a large number of memories and stories kept coming back to time just sitting around his back porch eating, drinking, talking, and telling jokes. Even those who initially got to know Mark only as recording artists for whom he was producing or engineering—Brooks Williams, John Austin, etc.—found themselves drawn into this world (as Brooks recalls in his song "Won't You Meet Me," written for Mark during the time when Mark was in a coma).

A similar connection can be made between their expressions and understandings of human creativity, which both Tolkien and Heard highly valued. We make (create), Tolkien wrote, "because we are made: and not only made, but made in the image and likeness of a Maker."[35] Mark wrote as the fourth point of that letter how the heresy of gnosticism was damaging the church's view of creativity.

> (4) . . . Platonic thought would here rob man of his creativity and even the appreciation of the same, a significant portion of the image of God. This is seen fairly clearly in some instances, the value of creative endeavors sometimes being denounced as unspiritual or prideful manifestations of "self" by the church. Warped, prideful misuse of creativity is indeed a familiar phenomenon. But does the existence of murder cause life to be less real? . . . There is surely an obvious lack of concerted effort at upholding the created validity of aesthetics within the church . . .

> Under Plato, a table cannot be admired at face value. Only the perfect concept of hypothetical (spiritual) tableness can be appreciated, and all physical embodiments of the concept are deemed imperfect, inferior, and even illusory in deference to the reality of the concept. When couched in the terminology of the Christian subculture, this thought may find its way into teaching in a form like, "A song is not to be appreciated. Only that which it expresses (the goodness of God, for example) can be appreciated as having value and justifying the existence of the song. The melody and the poetry are irrelevant and insignificant." This is a low view of creativity and a low view of the Creation. How sad that the beauty God has created as well as latent beauty expressible

through human hands and voices cannot be appreciated. How sad to wish a bird would preach rather than sing.[36]

IT'S NOT YOUR FAULT

Reading this letter, it is clear that Mark was not criticizing Christianity itself. Rather the opposite: in the tradition of Francis Schaeffer, he was defending Christianity against invasions from gnosticism and other heresies. Thus in his letter he encouraged the recipient to "Try to be patient with them [those in the church who are threatened by his questions and get nasty]."[37]

Mark's own criticisms of the church, however—of christendom, not Christianity—could be biting at times. It could be mildly veiled in imagery such as "Dancing at the Policeman's Ball," or it could be less subtle such as in his songs "Growing Up Blind," "I'm In Chains," "Holy War," or "We Believe So Well" from *Ashes and Light*:

> But we believe so well
>
> Don't we tell ourselves
>
> Don't we take exclusive pride that we abide so far from Hell
>
> We might laugh together
>
> But don't we cry alone
>
> For the ashes and the dust we've swept beneath the holy
>
> throne.

Again, Mark was not out to attack the church, but to encourage an awareness within it that would lead to change and spiritual growth. Like a prophet (though Mark would not have used such a word to describe himself) he was willing to make people uncomfortable, which is often a good thing.

Unfortunately, Mark found his "message" misunderstood, ignored, or even attacked. And so his criticism of numerous aspects of the subculture of christendom—a subculture that he felt had little to do with Christianity itself, or with Christ—as well as his efforts to distance himself from that subculture, continued to grow more vehement as he became more and more aware of its shortcomings. As many people noted, his biting commentary could have a negative side. Tom Howard recalls:

> He and I had lots of back-porch beer-swilling conversations about (you know) basically what is truth. Twenty-something kids, we're going to figure it out. I think Mark was a very complicated person: profoundly sensitive, and able to be scathingly dismissive. He had all the earmarks of a really brilliant artist and genius. He had really the full spectrum . . . [and] everybody that knew him and loved him and got anywhere close to him pretty much experienced the whole gamut at some point or another.

To say Mark was a "very complicated person" was certainly an understatement. What Tom might equally have pointed out was simply that Mark was human and imperfect. As is true with all of us, the better you knew him the more you saw his strengths as well as his weaknesses. Particularly later in his life, it seems, the closer you got to issues related to church subculture, the more likely you were to see creeping out the rare side of him that could be "scathingly dismissive."

Steve Hindalong was one of Mark's closer friends who experienced that caustic side in a painful way. The time came at the end of Mark's life. Steve had persuaded him to participate in his project, *At the Foot of the Cross*, contributing lead vocals to the song "My Redeemer Lives." Mark had been reluctant to agree—he was in the midst of releasing *Satellite Sky*, and still held out this hope that it would somehow break beyond the sub-culture of christendom. So he was nervous about taking a project that would too closely associate him with the CCM industry. He agreed to record the song, but when it came time to perform it at Cornerstone in 1992, he flatly refused.

Steve recalls the situation clearly.

> I was at Cornerstone. I was mad at him at the time. *At The Foot of the Cross* was being performed, and he wouldn't sing for it. One of the reasons he was booked at the festival was because they were trying to book the people who had sung on it so they could perform. Kate [Miner] came and performed, but for some reason Mark didn't want to do anything else. He was doing something with the Vigilantes [of Love]. Also, he thought his career was still going to become some secular thing. For some reason he wouldn't participate.

I was hurt about it, and was kind of mad . . . I didn't understand it. Sometimes he was so uptight about things. I said "All you got to do is stand there and sing 'My Redeemer Lives.'" But he was stubborn for whatever reason. Even to that last minute Kate was saying, "I'll talk to him. I'll get him to do it." [But in the end] we had to get somebody else.

This left in Steve's mind this strange sense of irony. "'My Redeemer Lives' is celebrated [as Mark's final recording]. They played it at his funeral. They played it at his grave. It became [famous as his] last vocal. But he wouldn't sing it at Cornerstone."

WE HAVE LET FREEDOM RING

1987, previously unreleased

We're free to see anything we want to see no matter what is there
imagination
We can find any fault we want to find as long as love is blind
imagination
We can tell any lie we want to tell as long as it's not true
imagination
You can hurt anyone you want to hurt as long as it's not you
imagination

Just another wild heart wrapped up in the role of predator
Untamed unchained unashamed unaware of danger

Run for your life we have let freedom ring'
Watch out for your heart we have let freedom ring
Pray for your soul we have let freedom ring

You can kill anything you want to kill-we know that war is hell
You can take any poison that will kill a member of your race
You can blow any bomb you want to blow as long as you've got votes
You can hang anyone you want to hang as long as you've got rope

Just another noble beast made drunk by the blood of the victim
Outrun overcome by another with a similar addiction

THE CRUEL PARADE

1987, previously unreleased

Check out the national pawn
He cries before he's hurt
He rants from dawn til dawn
He bleeds before he's cut
With a journalist's stance and a trenchcoat of beige
He's got an eye for compassion and a penchant for rage
He'll do anything

Here comes the cruel parade
Here comes the cruel parade (A reassuring charade)

Call out the National Guard
Call off the baby boom
Muster up the Nielson clan
Into the family room
I wonder what he'd do without the rumors of wars
He might know he's alive but he'd wonder what for
He'll do anything

Here comes the cruel parade
Here comes the cruel parade (A reassuring charade)

A little rural decay
A little urban crime
A little lunar soil
Some token peace of mind
Rome is afire he's got bellow to flame
Selling cereal and saccharin to the children of slaves
He'll do anything

Here comes the cruel parade
Here comes the cruel parade (A reassuring charade)

LETTING YOU DOWN

1988, previously unreleased

No-not another slowdance

I'll only make a fool of myself

I can take humiliation

But I'd rather take a walk around town

Come on

Let's have a conversation

I'll mutter and stumble on words

You try to draw me out

You will run when there's stories to tell

And somehow

I'm letting you down

I feel your eyes

A pair of blue knives

I'm letting you down

Do you want my blood?

I could offer you love

But I'm letting you down

I'm carrying a burden

I'd like to be laying it down

You could lift it from my shoulders

But you don't wanna have to carry it around and somehow

I'm letting you down

I feel your eyes

A pair of blue knives

I'm letting you down

Do you want my blood?

I could offer you love

But I'm letting you down

So many ways I can fail you

I get confused

And you have such unreasonable expectations

I'd like to be a superhero

I try to be an honorable sinner

Don't need another martyr

Try to make me into something I never could be

I'm letting you down

I feel your eyes

A pair of blue knives

I'm letting you down

Do you want my blood?

I could offer you love

But I'm letting you down

BECAUSE IS WHAT SHE SAYS

1988, previously unreleased

She can give you the time of day

If you'll hang on, hang on for a minute

There is so much she wants to say

If you'll hang on, hang on

Well I'm the one who takes that stuff

And she's the one who turns away

When the question is why

Because is what she says

Just because

There's that look in her eye

Because because oh yeah

Just because

She can steal you and sell your soul

Have you bought out, bought out in a minute

If there's a scalp that she wants to hold

She will hold on, hold on

Well I'm the one that's left for dead

And she's not even keeping score

When the question is why

Because is what she says

Just because

There's that curious smile

Because because oh yeah

Just because

And in the light of blackest night

She held me

Telling me lies

Please tell me why

Please tell me why

I would kiss her and say goodbye

If I could hold up, hold up for a minute

If I think for too long a while

This could go on, go on

So I'm the one who walks away

And she don't even know I'm gone

When the question is why

Because is what I'll say

Just because

It's not like I didn't try

Because because oh yeah

Just because

Mark in Elementary School

Mark at 2 yrs. old with his
first fish, in Georgia

Mark as a highschool senior.

Switzerland—hiking in the early 1980s.

A concert in Europe.

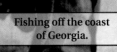
Fishing off the coast of Georgia.

Mark and Janet in the Sierra Nevada mountains.

Janet, Rebecca and Mark on their 15th anniversary.

Sequoia National forest.

L'Abri in Switzerland.

15th anniversary again.

Switzerland.

Mark and Rebecca at the zoo, 1989

Family with Susan (Mark's sister) in Albuquerque, NM, 1990.

Together in Saguaro National Park in Arizona, 1992.

Mark's parents, Jean and John Mark in Taos, NM, 1990.

Rebecca playing Mark's mandolin in Janet's lap.

Mark and Rebecca in the studio, 1992.

Tribal Opera

Dry Bones Dance

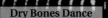

Second Hand

Satellite Sky

High Noon

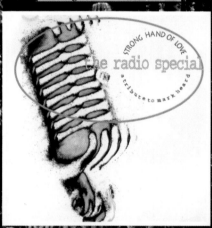

{5}

HAMMERS AND NAILS

I offer a couple of philosophical observations

on Mark Heard. He heard what a lot of other people

stopped hearing once they became Christians. He kept hearing the

cries of people who forgot their point of origin in the mind of God.

Mark never sacrificed the question for the answer, but gave them

both with paradoxical realism.

—John Fischer[38]

HAMMERS AND NAILS

1992, *Satellite Sky*

Fire in my shallows, sap of my soul

I'm hungry for mercy and thirsty for slack

Out in the outland, the flesh and the dust

Weight of the tired earth is breaking my back

Hope where I left it under the skin

Countenance of maidens, the stance of the laddies

The healing of old wounds, the trust of my kin,

The voices of children calling me daddy

Your love

Never can fail to pierce me

Hammers and nails

Rhythm of passion louder than Hell

Thunder of Heaven

Hammers and nails

Light in the dark eyes, coal into diamonds

Shelter from heavy skies, sand into pearls

Bread for the breathless, cloth for the fresh wounds

Order and chaos orbit the half-world

The taste of a color, the flavor of light

None but a blind man can measure the weight

I am a deaf-mute idle as statue

Music of hemispheres lost in the half-haze

Your love

Never can fail to pierce me

Hammers and nails
Rhythm of passion louder than Hell
Thunder of Heaven
Hammers and nails

Hum in the graveyard, whistle in the dark
Stains on the stained glass, pains in the heart
In the darkened corners love lies forgotten
In the heat of the moment it waits to be spotted
How can I slight you, how could I turn
How can you take it when I'm blind to your pain
The burning of fingers, the smoldering nerves
How can you take me back over and over again

Your love
Never can fail to pierce me
Hammers and nails
Rhythm of passion louder than Hell
Thunder of Heaven
Hammers and nails

THE THUNDER OF HEAVEN

In his book *Now and Then: A Memoir of Vocation,* Frederich Buechner describes a former seminar professor of his named James Muilenburg:

> "Every morning when you wake up," he used to say, "before you reaffirm your faith in the majesty of a loving God, before you say I believe for another day, read the Daily News with its record of the latest crimes and tragedies of mankind and then see if you can honestly say it again." He was a fool in the sense that he didn't or couldn't or wouldn't resolve, intellectualize, evade, the tensions of his faith, but lived those tensions out, torn almost in two by them at times. His faith was not a seamless garment but a ragged garment with the seams showing, the tears showing, a garment that he clutched about him like a man in a storm.[39]

When I read those words, I immediately thought of Mark Heard. He was a man who fit Buechner's description of Professor Muilenburg: a man who felt the tensions of living in a fallen world while clinging still to a profound faith. Mark had felt the Crucial Revelation—the incarnation of his Creator—and yet he lived his life at the "blind intersection" where the "broad streets of the heart and the day to day meet." Even the simple fact that the local playground had padlocks and chains on the gates[40] caused him grief. In his letter about gnosticism that was quoted in the previous chapter, Mark wrote:

> . . . the Bible certainly does not teach this [gnosticism], although it has crept into the church unnoticed. You may hear, "Don't bother crying about your brother's death. To be in heaven is much better than to live on earth, so envy him." This is Platonic thought. The Biblical response would be, "Cry and grieve that death has taken your brother. Cry that it exists, that it has broken unwelcome into God's creation. But know that God cries too, and hang on, if you can, to the hope He has revealed to us that He has defeated death ultimately."

Unlike the beliefs of the gnostics, the spiritual realm did not invalidate the physical for Mark. He felt "circumstance crashing through his walls like a train." He was, in his own words, a "profane saint" living out his penance. His refusal to blind himself to the struggles and pains of the world around him was certainly evident in his songwriting.

As Dan Russell commented to me: "Because of [Mark's] honesty, he wasn't able to fake a smile or 'testify' on cue . . . This incredibly gifted, talented, funny, intelligent, loving, compassionate man was cursed to know too much, and he was ultimately unwilling to lie about the truth that scorched his soul." As a result, there were many who felt that his songs were too depressing. "He wasn't that popular with the yet-to-be-weaned christian subculture," Dan continued. "This youth group club christian environment might only have made sense for Mark when he was in college. Mark couldn't survive a subculture that oversimplified life and sought to make everything safe, cute, and neat."

Because Mark didn't make everything safe, cute, and neat—because he expressed his doubts, confusion, and frustrations, and because some of these frustrations were directed at elements within the christian subculture—some even questioned whether or not Mark could possibly have any Christian faith at all. Some suggested that by the time of his last three albums he had abandoned any faith he once had. Yet from references to Heaven's hammers being louder than those of Hell,[41] to the expectant prayer for the "waiting wind of Gabriel [to] blow soon upon these hollow bones,"[42] to the affirmation that "it takes more than your passion and more than your pain for the rock of forgiveness to melt in the rain,"[43] to the "miraculous circumstance where the blind ones see and the dry bones dance,"[44] there is clear evidence in those final three albums of a Christian world view, and specifically of a Christian hope.

Indeed, for many of his fans, those affirmations of faith meant all the more, precisely because they *did* come from somebody who didn't "evade the tensions of his faith," but lived them out despite the heavy cost to himself. As Pat Terry aptly commented:

> Quite frankly, when you listen to these songs—especially the later albums, which were the best albums of his career, there's no doubt about that—when you listen to these songs, some of those songs were very painful for me to listen to because I hear his struggles in those things. Him dealing with those issues and expressing them in his music was not something that was particularly fulfilling and made him feel good. It just expressed the level of angst in him. People sometimes have a tendency to overlook how human he was. When he was singing about difficult things, he was feeling those difficult things. It was hard. It did

take a toll on him physically and emotionally.

Still, Mark could "read the daily news with its record of the latest crimes and tragedies of mankind" and in the end honestly cling to his faith. He heard the pounding of Hell's hammers. But he heard the pounding of Heaven's hammers too. And in the end, he knew that the thunder of Heaven was the louder. Thus in his music he was able, in his own words, "to conjure the magic of something good waiting around the corner, over the hill, tomorrow, on the morning of the resurrection."

In fact, Mark did precisely what he recommended in his letter: he cried and he grieved, but he held onto the hope. And so, as odd or incomprehensible as it seems to some, for many people Mark's music has always been more (and not less) encouraging because of the pain and grief that it communicates. When he communicates a message of hope, it is not blind or ignoring the problems of the world. Rather, he recognized all the worst of the world and yet still was able to claim the hope despite that.

"It's like [his song] 'Heart of Hearts,'" Tom Howard comments. "I mean, he's seen all this, and where it brought him was to his knees. And I truly see that in that man."

SHOOT FROM THE HEART AGAIN

Perhaps it was Mark's aversion to the false spirituality that he associated with gnosticism that led him to be so caustic toward anything that struck him as phoniness within the church. As Pat Terry commented:

> I think what he valued more than anything was honesty. Honesty was the hallmark of what he did. That's what he encouraged other people to do—to be honest. The cool thing with what Mark accomplished was that, with everything that was so great about him as a person, and then also with his foibles . . .

> I think the thing that he struggled with, and the thing that was his biggest challenge, was to continue to write honest songs in the context of a musical industry that was about marketing. That's hard to do. That's what he did, and that's what he encouraged others to do.

> His achievement to me was that he wrote honest music as a very normal guy. I think that's how he would want people to know him.

Randy Stonehill recalls a show he did with Mark in Houston. The promoter, who was helping to coordinate the event, gathered the band members around backstage before the concert. "He was like a football coach who was gonna give the team a pep talk," Randy recalls. He had them all holding hands in a circle, and then he started praying, "obviously doing it for our benefit to impress us or something." One by one, people were praying in a circle, and everyone had their heads bowed and their eyes closed. It was hokey, Randy thought, but he figured he'd just try to speak from the heart. But then it was Mark's turn.

> There was this awkward silence and then all of a sudden he just started whistling the theme to Mayberry RFD. It was like he just couldn't resist. He just had to bust the moment. I thought, "This is certainly the wrong thing to do. He's not going to be invited back." But at the same time, for him it was like the most honest thing he could do in the moment. And everybody was [simultaneously] cringing [but also] acknowledging that somebody had to pop the b.s. bubble and laughing at the same time.

This sort of story about Mark abounds. Even in his own journal, he acknowledges an occasion where he essentially walked away from a record contract simply because he refused to say something that the record executive wanted him to say in the way he wanted Mark to say it.

> All he wanted was to hear me use the lingo, recite the mantras of evangelical musicians, kids who have been made to feel guilty using their musical abilities, and who, as a result, must justify their talents with post-Jesus movement creeds—formula statements that are as culturally nebulous and stale as the Victorian ones against which that movement originally cried out.

> He tried several more times to get me to just say the words. I said that I would make it a point not to say those particular words, if for no other reason than to get him to think about what they meant.

> Being a smart person, he knows I would have to do interviews to sell records for him, and that in those interviews, I would be asked the same types of questions, and I would be expected to toe the party line and echo the same litanies—make the "comforting noise," as McLuhan put it.

I told him I just want to write some more songs and put them on tape. I figure the content of the songs and how I choose to answer for myself is my business. He says he is sorry, even cut to the heart, but he cannot and will not sign me, as, alas, I cannot say the things he wanted to hear. [From "Politics" starting p.187]

How does a fan of Mark's respond to a story like this?

"I saw Mark do stuff like that," Randy Stonehill recalls. "Just sort of dummy up in the middle of radio interviews and things, just because he was so exasperated by the shallowness of the interviewer."

A comment from Dan Russell puts the episode in a larger context:

In an effort to build a larger audience, he was cornered a few times and asked to compromise his integrity to fit some quick read, cliché, slug line promotional campaign . . . but couldn't swallow it. His faith could never be an adjective. This was fuel for his depression . . . one that he struggled with from time to time.

He couldn't survive the subculture and from 1986 forward he was headed away from it.

Mark was certainly aware that this was dangerous to his career, at least in terms of recording contracts, radio airplay, and commercial success. "Man," he'd say to Randy, bemoaning his own inability to play the game, "That's why you'll have more career longevity than I will. That's why you're more liked than I am. Because you can kind of roll with the punches."[45]

Aware of the danger, yes, but still unwilling to change. Was it stubbornness, or integrity? Maybe both. Randy often felt—and it was a frustrating feeling—that if Mark had just gone along with the game a little bit, he would have been free to perform his music without changing it. If he had just been willing simply to say one or two sentences the way the record company executive wanted him to say them, it would have worked out fine, at least in terms of commercial success. It may well be thoughts like this that prompted the line in "Big Wheels Roll":

He tells himself that they're lame and weak

but he only has himself to blame.

But Mark despised the phoniness. He could not just pretend.

All talk and no touch

And I just wanna be real

"He hated all that: those christian concerts," reflects Tim Alderson. One of Mark's closest friends, as well as somebody who worked with him professionally, Tim had many chances to witness Mark in these situations.

> [When performing a concert] in the regular music business, what you really are when you're a band trying to make it is a way to sell beer. I mean, they bring in a band to make noise to make people buy booze. And that's really what the music business is about. And the christian music business is about the same way, except they're selling something different. And Mark hated being a come-on for a preacher, you know? It's like, the bait being switched. You bring a music act in and you pretend like you're doing something for the kids and then get a captive audience and then preach to them. And he hated being used that way.

In a 1987 interview with Milo Carter for *Newsound* Magazine, while discussing some of the motivation behind his song "How to Grow Up Big and Strong," Mark made an interesting comment about how individual human worth seems always under attack, no matter what type of society one lives in. Though the context of that comment is very different from that of the present chapter, the thoughts Mark shared are profound and informative:

> You can see it in the capitalist systems of the world where it doesn't matter whose toes you step on just as long as you survive, as long as you're the fittest, as long as your financial genes dominate the gene pool; you can see it in the communist societies where it's "our people must survive, therefore you, as the person, are going to have to make sacrifices;" you can see it in the Nazi ideas about genetic engineering for the good of the state. In all of these instances the value of the individual human is subjugated to the direction of the larger whole.[46]

Pat Terry summarized as follows:

> He hated [presumption] because he really, really believed in the value and worth of the individual. He felt like, if you were made in God's image, then in-and-of-itself that was enough. That

has worth and value. He always celebrated that. In the Christian community, if you really feel that and believe that to the extent that Mark did—he really lived it—then you get beat up. It's tough. For Mark it was like he could only go so far and he ran out of patience.

And so, in the final analysis, Randy's overriding impression from his whole history with Mark was a "sense of great integrity and honor about him."

I JUST WANNA BE REAL

As Mark and Randy knew, Mark's stubbornness and integrity—his aversion to phoniness, and his quickness to point it out even at inopportune times—was certainly detrimental to his career (at least from the point of view of financial success). And yet many friends and fans were deeply encouraged by Mark's integrity to be more real and authentic themselves.

Randy remembers sitting down with Mark before recording *Return to Paradise*, which Mark was producing. Mark was telling him:

> Now Randy, you know you're considered one of the pioneers of the genre, and you know you sing very well. Gosh, I mean the audience knows it, you know it, the public knows it, and record companies know it. So just do me a favor, okay? When you get in front of the microphone, don't sing to me.

Randy sat back, half-confused and half-insulted, as Mark gritted his teeth and explained what he meant.

> Randy, just don't get caught up in the mechanics of hearing how cool your voice sounds, because if you do that it will just destroy it. When you step outside the moment, and you're just worrying about the notes, you actually undermine the very thing you're trying to do. Just let the song tell the story. If you do that, then the song will breathe; then it will have life. Don't worry about your chops.

Randy got red in the face because on the one level it was insulting. At another level, however, he knew it was true and that it was good advice. Mark was calling him to make his performance more about honesty and integrity and just being real than about musicality.

Randy had a similar experience when he was preparing to record *Wonderama*, although this time it had more to do with the writing of songs than the performance. There was a brief period when he thought Mark would be producing *Wonderama*, and so he brought about eighteen songs over to his house one afternoon, and over about a two hour period proceeded to play through them all. All the while, Mark just sat on his rocking chair, his big old fluffy cat, Chester, in his lap, making notes on his yellow legal pad. When Randy was done, he expected Mark to pick about twelve songs from the list, suggest how they'd need to tighten them up, or what to add to them to fill them out. Instead, to Randy's shock, Mark looked at him and said, "Well those are pretty good. But you know what you need to do now? You need to go and write some Randy Stonehill songs."

Again, Randy got red in the face with panic. "Mark, I just played you eighteen songs. We are sixty days out from the start of production. Are you telling me I don't have a record here?"

"No, no," Mark replied. "You could make a record. But it wouldn't be the right one. You gotta keep stretching for the next high water mark with every record. You can't just crank these out."

Randy could sense the integrity and care in what Mark was saying. Behind the spoken words, he could hear the message, *Randy, life is short. We're doing this as unto the Lord. Keeping digging in, man, you know?* He needed to be more real and more authentic. Still, that didn't make him feel any more secure about the fact that he had two months until the start of recording. How would he accomplish it?

But then Mark's voice softened. Perhaps he saw the panic in Randy's expression, or the sheer terror in his eyes. In any case, Mark's next comment showed his humor, kindness, love, and artistic insight all at the same time. "Hey man. Don't worry about it. I mean, you can do it. After all, you are him." It was moments like these that probably prompted Pierce Pettis' reflection that Mark was "the single funniest person I ever met, and one of the most sincere."

And Randy, in the midst of his sputtering, had to laugh. Nobody had ever said to him, *Hey man, don't panic. Go write some real Randy Stonehill songs. You can do it. After all, you are him.* As a result, he ended up throwing out eighty-percent of the material and writing (or co-writing with Terry Taylor) what he considers one of the strongest records of his career in terms of the material.

IT'S NOTHING PERSONAL
1987, previously unreleased

It's not your race

It's not your creed

It's not your manners or philosophy

It's just the way you walk

The way you talk

The way you try to capture me

    Don't want you close to me

    How can I make you see ooooh

It's nothing personal (it's just the way I feel)

It's nothing personal (it's just the way it is)

It's nothing personal

It's just you

    It's nothing personal

It's not your face

It's not your job

It's not your family that scares me so

It's just the way you think

The way you act

The shambles of your self-control

It's not the way you smile

The way you laugh

That makes me want to slap your face

It's just the way you've been

The way you are

And who you underestimate

LOOK OVER YOUR SHOULDER

1991, Second Hand

Look over your shoulder and tell me what's coming

Tell me what is the bogey that you're so afraid of

The eyes in the back of our heads can persuade

That just for the moment mercy has swayed

Look over your shoulder and tell me what's coming

Look into your sad eyes and tell me what you see

What is left of the child who is hiding behind them

Who longs to be laughing in places of light

Who knows that the morning will follow the night

Look into your sad eyes and tell me what you see

If you must be afraid be afraid of yourself

For being afraid of the fear you have felt

You will weather well in a climate of love

It takes more than your passion and more than your pain

For the rock of forgiveness to melt in the rain

Look over your shoulder and tell me what's coming

Look into your sad eyes and tell me what you see

Look over your shoulder and tell me what's coming

THAT PRETTY YOUNG THING

1988, previously unreleased

She was a goddess with eyes like a dove

I offered up my confessions of love

I could imagine the prize of her touch

Imagination is never enough

That pretty young thing

That pretty young thing

Dashed every hope that I had to my name

That pretty young thing

That pretty young girl

She was everything I could want in this world

She was a jewel unbearably rare

Wore all the rays of the sun in her hair

I could go for days on the promise of one kiss

I could wait forever and that's what I did

That pretty young thing

That pretty young thing

Dashed every hope that I had to my name

That pretty young thing

That pretty young girl

She was everything I could want in this world

She was an angel unearthly and fair

I had to know everything about her

I still remember what time won't erase

She has forgotten my name and my face

That pretty young thing

That pretty young thing

Dashed every hope that I had to my name

That pretty young thing

That pretty young girl

She was everything I could want in this world

HOLE IN MY HEART

1987, previously unreleased

I'll never get over you

You're a dream in the strobe of a flickering street light

Oh what can I say to you

When there's nothing to say and it's after midnight

I'd do about anything to keep a love from becoming so obsolete

I'll never be able to turn to face this music and take this heat

I don't want to lose you, oh no

But here I stand just letting you go

There's a hole in my heart where there used to be love

There is water and ice where there used to be blood

And where there used to be fire there's a hollow vacuum

There's a hole in my life where there used to be you

You'd gotten me used to feeling how a heart can melt in a warm embrace

I never will understand how the same turns brittle and breaks in pieces

I'd do about anything to wake up and discover this is all just a nightmare

But you're gone and I'm wide awake

Left to bite this bullet and pull my hair

WHEN YOU'VE MADE YOUR NAME

1987, previously unreleased

Before you go and turn this town upside down

Remember why kings wear their crowns with their frowns

And when you see your name in lights

Wonder if the world will be better

When you've made your name

And you've left your mark

When you walk on the public sea remember me

It can drown you by degrees and then recede

And when you're standing in that glow

I hope that you will still hear your heart beat

When you can have anything you want as your wage

Just keep the things that can't be bought and will not change

And as you're marching off to war

I hope that you'll remember what love is

STRONG HAND OF LOVE

1987, *Dry Bones Dance*

Down peppers the rain from a clear blue sky

Down trickles a tear on a youthful face

Feeling in haste, wondering why

Up struggles the sun from a wounded night

Out venture our hearts in their silent shrouds

Trying to ignite but wondering how

We can laugh and we can cry

And never see the strong hand of love hidden in the shadows

We can dance and we can sigh

And never see the strong hand of love hidden in the shadows

Young dreamers explode like popped balloons

Some kind of emotional rodeo

Learning too slow and acting too soon

Time marches away like a lost platoon

We gracefully age as we feel the weight

Of loving too late and leaving too soon

We can laugh and we can cry

And never see the strong hand of love hidden in the shadows

We can dance and we can sigh

And never see the strong hand of love hidden in the shadows

LOOKING FOR A MOONRISE

1989, previously unreleased
Mark Heard and Kate Miner
©1989 Ideola music/Dwinell music

Through the curtain of the setting sun

I wonder where the light is shining

And where will you be next

I don't know

In following shadows and lights

Looking there for you

But I've only succeeded

In blinding my eyes

And I'm looking for a moonrise

For a constant in the sunless sky

Waiting for a moonrise

It will rise . . .

Horizon turns to gold and you wait

For me on the edge and I strain

For one sweet sight

One sweet sight

Your breath is the wind that blows

Breathe on me and I will go

Toward the fire it fans

Move towards the fire

And I'm looking for a moonrise

For a constant in the sunless sky

Waiting for a moonrise

It will rise . . .

South of the north star

And north of the southern cross

Someplace east of Eden

Points of silver blue

Shine into my soul

Through the curtain of the setting sun

I wonder where the light is shining

And where I'll see you next

I don't know

Heaven holds the heat of your love

Cinders speak with a radiant pulse

Oh burn bright

Burn bright

And I'm looking for a moonrise

For a constant in the sunless sky

Waiting for a moonrise

It will rise . . .

LONELY ROAD

1989, *Dry Bones Dance*

Not taking note of the fools or the wise

Being a pawn of time and chance

Not making vows when the flood waters rise

Is simpler than nails through the hands

Being a slave to the sultans of grief

Keeping the hand to the plow

Being held captive to public belief

Is easier than thorns through the brow

And it's a lonely road

And it's a lonely road

And it's a lonely road

That the Son of Man walks down

Being immune to the war of the heart

And never wondering why

To bury the conflict deep in the dark

Is safer that spears through the side

And it's a lonely road

And it's a lonely road

And it's a lonely road

That the Son of Man walks down

For him who burns with a creed and a flame

Words are as smoke on the wind

Some kind of volatile helplessness reigns

And can't fill the hearts of his kin

To go and enlighten the doomed and unwashed
Seized with the art of sacrifice
To carry the weight of a martyr-at-large
Is easier than giving your life

And it's a lonely road
And it's a lonely road
And it's a lonely road
That the Son of Man walks down

[Mark Heard, A dock in Maine.]

{6}

THE FRICTION BORN OF LIVING

"...a cry to God about how much I hate the bad

things and how much I love the good things."

—Mark Heard

"There was a warmth about him but at the same time,

a sort of an undercurrent in his approach to the world. He played it pretty

close to the vest. You didn't really get to know him too terribly well. There

were precious few people that really got behind his eyes and got to know him.

Sometimes, even through all the years we toured together—even for all the years

I'd known him—I didn't know if he really liked me."

—Randy Stonehill

WORRY TOO MUCH

1991, *Second Hand*

It's the demolition derby

It's the sport of the hunt

Proud tribe in full war-dance

It's the slow smile that the bully gives the runt

It's the force of inertia

It's the lack of constraint

It's the children out playing in the rock garden

All dolled-up in black hats and war paint

Sometimes it feels like bars of steel

I cannot bend with my hands

Oh—I worry too much

Somebody told me that I worry too much

It's these sandpaper eyes

It's the way they rub the lustre from what is seen

It's the way we tell ourselves that all these things

are normal

Til we can't remember what we mean

It's the flicker of our flames

It's the friction born of living

It's the way we beat a hot retreat

And heave our smoking guns into the river

Sometimes it feels like bars of steel

I cannot bend with my hands

Oh—I worry too much

Somebody told me that I worry too much

It's the quick-step march of history
The vanity of nations
It's the way there'll be no muffled drums
To mark the passage of my generation
It's the children of my children
It's the lambs born in innocence
It's wondering if the good I know
Will last to be seen by the eyes of the little ones

Sometimes it feels like bars of steel
I cannot bend with my hands
Oh—I worry too much
Somebody told me that I worry too much

HAVE MY SENSES TAKEN LEAVE? I DOUBT IF YOU'D KNOW.

As I worked on this book, some of the stories I heard about Mark could only make me laugh. Over the course of my interviews, other than "passionate" and "honest," the word I most often heard associated with Mark was "idiosyncratic." As Steve Hindalong describes it:

> His idiosyncrasies are what we always talk about. His neurosis. He'd be sitting at a restaurant and start scratching himself and say: "I wonder what kind of dish detergent they're using in there." And perfume really bothered him. He'd say: "Is so-and-so coming today because her perfume always comes into the room before she does."
>
> One time a bee comes into the studio and he says: "If that bee stings me, don't call the doctor, don't call the ambulance, don't do anything, because I'll be dead." I guess he was allergic to bees.

Stories about recording sessions with Mark abound, especially about his little homemade studio that began in the famed "ice-cream truck" and eventually moved to a little shed behind his house. His recording console came from Trident in London, and had previously been used to record the Rolling Stones' "Let it Bleed."[47] When Mark first acquired it and was cleaning it out, he found a bunch of marijuana seeds in it.

"You'll probably be scared when you see it. It's like half a shed," he told John Austin, as they prepared to start recording *The Embarrassing Young*. John wasn't scared, but he still finds it hard to believe that they ever fit David Miner's stand-up bass in there. Mark, however, had a way of making it work, whether in the shed, or even before that in the even-smaller ice-cream truck. As Tom Howard tells:

> There's a funny thing about him singing his songs. He was such a self-made person—such a Renaissance man. He had to do everything by himself . . . right up until he died. He had that goofy ice-cream truck of a recording studio. And he worked out a physical position that he could get into, and work some faders with his feet, and lean back almost in a prone position so he could work, and see controls, and turn machines on and off, and punch in. It was hilarious. He demonstrated to me one afternoon how he sang these songs. I cracked up. Here he was, almost lying

flat, on this chair. And he got into some position where he felt like the mike placement was right. He was a total contortionist. It was funny.

When I first visited the Heard's house with my brother several years ago, I remember Janet showing me the studio (after it had moved to the shed). Still stuck against the wall near the door were several strips of masking tape, each of which had, at different times, been used to label the various channels on the console for the recordings he had engineered: drums, snare, tom, high-hat, lead vocals, bass, etc. And at the end of each strip of tape was also scrawled the name of the artist and album. As I studied the strips more closely, I realized (with a little awe) that some of my favorite albums had been recorded or mixed in that tiny little studio.

Included among those albums were a few of Mark's own, recorded in the same eccentric fashion as the numerous albums he recorded for other people. "He only took about two weeks a year to do his records," John Austin shares, "what he called taking his yearly 'creative dump.'" Buddy Miller got to take part in one of these "yearly dumps," and to watch Mark at work on *Second Hand*:

> I remember telling Mark [shortly after we met that] I was an admirer of his music, and if he needed a hand recording just let me know. And it's funny because it wasn't very long after that I get a call out of the blue. "I'll be doing a new record. Want to help engineer?"
>
> I didn't think he'd be calling me. I thought he had his way of doing things well worked out. I said "sure." I went up there one morning to his house. Half of his garage he'd use for storage and the other half [for recording]. It was a tiny little area. I can't believe he made records in there. There wasn't enough room for two people in there. But there was a door between the tiny part of the room where the recorder and the board was and the back part of the room where the amp was, and he sat back there. We went into the house, and had a cup of coffee or something. Then we went out back. He took out his book, where he had all his song possibilities in it. And he just starts turning the pages.
>
> "We'll do that one," he says, turning the pages. "I guess we'll do this one." Just picking out the songs. And there's tons of songs to choose from. And he just . . . dit dit dit dit . . . he picked out his

record right then—what he was going to record . . .

He was pretty well organized I guess—at least more so than me—cause he'd look at the song title and then turn and find a cassette that had the song on it. He'd listen to the original, and he'd get a tempo. Then he'd go in the back part of the room, and I'd be in the front, and I'd engineer for him. All I thought, while this was going down—because I couldn't tell what he was doing from what was in his head about how it would turn into a record—I was thinking, "This is going to be the first Mark Heard record that's no good." It didn't make any sense to me the way he was working.

I wasn't a great engineer. And I'm still not. And I'd be punching in things, and I'd mess up on a punch. He'd say, "Don't worry about it. This is how I figure out where to put my percussion. I put my percussion on the bad punches."

The last album Mark produced before his death was the debut CD of Harrod and Funck, *Dreams of the Color Blind*. Of those two weeks spent recording with Mark, Jason Harrod recalls,

It was a giddy, heady experience—my first time west of Wisconsin, and my first time in a "real" studio. I had just turned twenty. Mark was very kind, funny, and wryly matter-of-fact. "Your girlfriends will hate this record, because it won't sound like your demos," he said. He said we sounded like "Simon and Garfunkel on drugs" and kept encouraging us to write a "hit": something for the radio. So every day, we'd go home from the studio and rack our brains, trying to write something a little more accessible. Next day, we'd show up, guitars in tow, and play what we had written. "Nice song," he'd say, "but it's not a hit." Of course, this was all a bit tongue-in-cheek, and he'd say, "don't worry, I've never written a hit either."

There was undeniably a creative aspect to all of this. "One of his trademarks was 'swamp gas,' Jason remembers. It "was basically guitar feed-back put down as a 'pad.' This 'swamp gas' was all over the record and kind of gave it its spacious, ambient feel."

"Mark may have referred to himself as an 'old maid' in the studio," Dan Russell remarks, "but the truth is, he was anything but. He was inventive, creative, quick-thinking, and a great technical engineer."

Mark was also pretty set in his ways, and particular about how he did things in the studio. He had a goal, and the goal was authenticity. Whether he was recording his own music, or producing somebody else, it wasn't ultimately about playing a bunch of notes perfectly, but much more about capturing the passion of the music, and about keeping it real in the studio. When recording a song, he would record as much live as possible. When he couldn't record live, he would start with vocal and guitar and build everything around that. In John Austin's words, Mark wanted the music to be:

> . . . still hanging on to the singer and the song . . . [to] keep the record feeling as human as possible, no matter what instruments are used . . . His thinking was that this quality of immediacy or expressiveness was lost after the third or fourth vocal take. I think he's right. Music is not about perfection; it's about human expressiveness.

Jason and Brian discovered this the hard way. Jason describes the scene one day when they questioned Mark's approach:

> I was perhaps over-protective of our songs, and questioned the quality of a lot of the takes (after all, for our demos, Brian and I spent hours hunkered over Brian's four-track, getting every take just right). After one vocal take, I told Mark I thought the sound needed to be more "punchy." After a moment of silence, he looked at me and said, "Do you want to produce this f—ing thing? Cause if you do, I'll give you your money back and you can go home right now." All the blood drained out of Brian's face.

As an aside to this story, it must be noted that Mark applied that approach to himself as well. When he was recording *Second Hand*, he woke up one day sick with the flu, and decided to do all the vocals right then while he was sick.[48] Anyway, ten years later, Jason can laugh at the memory, especially at the next line out of Mark's mouth which was vintage Mark Heard stuff: "Don't worry. I still like you. I'd go bowling with you any time." As to the effect on Jason at the time? "After that, I trusted him a bit more."

Being on the road with Mark could also be crazy, due to his idiosyncrasies, which were not always benign. Steve Hindalong also remembers a tour he did with Mark in Holland.

There was this smoke machine going: the rock fog smoke machine [for special effects]. Mark said, "Don't use that fog machine."

[But the concert promoters] said, "We gotta use the fog machine." It was Holland. They barely spoke English. [So the concert starts and] the smog machine was going crazy. [Mark's] obsessed with that [machine] and was screaming in-between licks: "Turn off the fog! Turn off the smoke machine!"

I think they thought he was saying, "More smoke. More smoke," (because they kept putting out more smoke. If anything, they turned it up higher). I'm just playing drums in the middle of a cloud. [Mark] was very upset. He's worked himself into a frenzy over it. At the end of the gig he collapses on the drum monitor. Faints. Finally they help him off, and he's saying, "I feel like somebody hit me in the back of the head with a hammer." So the whole gig was this battle. We thought it was a great gig, and he's just going nuts.

The craziness of touring was not always due to any of Mark's peculiarities, however. "He and I were always going up to a gig in New Hampshire or something," recalls Joel Russell, "and we were always two or three hours late because we were stuck in a snowdrift, or in some roadside joint. And then you get to the gig and are literally walking right on [to stage] hoping that someone set up the mic and tuned something."

LOOK OVER YOUR SHOULDER

Mark's faith—or rather his *expression* of faith—also had its idiosyncrasies. He was a Christian, and by the accounts of everybody who knew him his faith was very important. Yet in his adult life he did not go to church. In fact, he was quite adamant in his refusal to attend church, or to have much of anything to do with any aspect of christian culture.

For some of Mark's friends, this was an occasional source of tension. "I remember one of the few times that I felt a frost come between us," Tom Howard recalls. "I was going to some kind of men's Bible study or something in Pasadena. And one evening I was at his house and I invited him to come and teach there. 'I can't go there,' he said. 'I can't do that.' I've never seen him so put off in my life." Tom sensed such a strong reaction that he wanted to probe a little bit further, but Mark didn't really want to talk about it. And Tom was not the only one to experience such a reaction. Several of his other friends and acquaintances had similar encounters. Those who risked pressing the issue were met with rather adamant responses, and in some cases experienced barriers creeping into their friendships.

Why such a strong reaction from Mark? Nearly everybody I spoke with who was close to him had to deal with this issue at one point or another in their relationship, and yet it was the most difficult topic to broach in the course of my interviews. Many of those I spoke with saw the merit in Mark's rejection of certain cultural-political aspects of the church and christendom. Yet they wondered, as did I, how Mark could turn so completely away from the church and still cling to a profound Christian faith?

Answers to this question were not simple, and I'm sure it would be a mistake to assume I found all of the issues, or that I understood all the complexities of those issues I did uncover. Nonetheless, over the course of several interviews, several contributing factors seemed to emerge to form a clearer picture.

The most obvious answer was that some damage had been done to Mark at an institutional level. Certainly his experiences in the contemporary christian music recording industry did nothing to endear Mark to christian subculture, nor did many of his experiences performing in so-called christian venues. When you read from his journals—especially "Politics" [see p.187] and "On Tour, January, 1979" [see p.189]—it is easy to see how deeply he was wounded at times. Even in the course of doing interviews for radio and magazines, he felt himself being questioned and doubted. As he wrote in "Reading Between The Questions," [see p.192] "I can't count the number of times I have felt hurt inside—that it couldn't just be accepted that I was a Christian—that I had to prove it on their terms and with their words."

The issue did not seem to be Mark's ego at all. He was sensitive to the whole scene, including how it affected younger new artists. Speaking of how he felt recording artists in general (and not just himself) were being treated by the industry, he added, "It's sad that the Christian music environment has not given these musicians enough of a feeling of self-worth to the point that they feel they must hide their identity on the fringes and emulate some other pop phenomenon in order to justify their musicianship."

There were hints, however, that some of Mark's response to the church may have come from an even earlier part of his life. Tom Howard took a reluctant stab at elucidating this:

> I have kind of that feeling that he was like one of the golden
> boys in his youth group or something, and he had great
> expectations which underneath it all he didn't trust. He didn't
> trust the motivations. I just think he felt totally kind of throttled
> into some role that he never had any resonance with.

Among other things, Mark's church background growing up may
have made him feel uncomfortable asking the myriad of spiritual and
philosophical questions he had. It was not an issue of an unhappy home
life. Mark had a very happy home, and a great relationship with his parents.
John, his father, had a notorious laugh which Mark reminisces about in
"Why, Mama, Why?" associating that laugh with the early time of his life
before the world became so painful.

> Why do I lie awake at night
>
> And think back just as far as I can
>
> To the sound of my father's laugh outdoors
>
> Before I could fashion my poverty
>
> Before I distrusted the night
>
> Those are the times I live for tonight

"[Mark's] dad was a great guy," Chuck Long recalls. "A true Southern
gentlemen in the best sense of that word. He loved to have a good time,
and he was a great storyteller, and Mark got a lot of that from his dad. They
loved jokes. His dad loved jokes, and Mark loved jokes too."

Rather, this gets us back to a subject explored earlier: what Pat Terry and
Chuck Long described as a guilt-laden Southern version of Christianity,
and more generally a presumptuousness that they encountered in many
evangelical communities. As Pat said, people will find out that they share
with you a common belief in a resurrected Christ, and because of that one
shared belief they presume upon your thinking in a myriad of other issues.
It was Pat's belief that Mark "found that very difficult to deal with, because
if you're an artist then your whole thing is to try to somehow get down
inside yourself and find out how *you* feel about something and express
that." Mark found it very uncomfortable to walk into someplace and have

somebody presume they knew him.

It was not until Mark went to L'Abri—which certainly looked nothing like what Mark associated with the traditional Christian church—that he found an environment in which he could ask questions without his faith being doubted. "I think L'Abri—his L'Abri experience—probably was a pivotal point for him just on an intellectual level," Tom Howard went on. "And then his experience in Los Angeles kind of capped it off."

A second issue that was certainly an obstacle to Mark's involvement in church had to do with doctrinal concerns. As I mentioned earlier, Mark felt that gnosticism had crept into the church and was doing considerable damage through a corrupting of Christian doctrine. One area in particular where this would have been deeply troubling to Mark was the devaluation of art and creativity. It would be difficult for an artist as gifted as he was to be a part of a congregation that wished "a bird would preach rather than sing."

Similarly, Mark's experience with the church was that it devalued the mind and intellectual pursuits—again, as a result of the influence of gnosticism corrupting true Christian doctrine. "Under gnostic presuppositions," he wrote, "the next part of us to go is rationality, the validity of the human reasoning process."

Janet commented on this aspect of Mark's faith. "I think he just wasn't comfortable in a typical church. If he could have been challenged intellectually, it would have been a different thing, but the typical church [didn't provide that]."

Joel Russell saw the same thing at work. "It wasn't only those bad christian gigs at churches. It was a lot of bad theology. He was so quick to point out that theology, and he was such a thinker. [He wasn't able to find] the kind of [teacher] who would really truly nurture and inspire the soul."

As Janet concluded, "with the people thinking about who knows what, he couldn't just focus on going and trying to listen to the pastor. There was just too much going on around that disturbed him too much to be able to get involved."

IT TAKES MORE THAN YOUR PASSION AND MORE THAN YOUR PAIN

As important as these previous issues were, there was another factor contributing to Mark's disassociation with the organized church. This last issue was perhaps the most significant, though it was only after Mark's death that some of his friends began to speculate aloud. At Mark's funeral in Macon, Pat Terry made a comment that maybe struck the nail closest to the head:[49] "Mark Heard did not have the filtering system that most other people have: the filter that makes it so that you don't take in everybody's shit. Of everybody I know, Mark was most lacking in that. He took it in. I think it fried him. It hurt him."

Randy Stonehill expressed it in a similar way.

> Living on the planet was so hard for him. I always had the feeling that he was a man who was never really comfortable being here. He loved his wife. He loved his daughter. He loved his friends. He loved music. But man, it was almost like his radar was too sensitive and he just couldn't filter out stuff, you know? There was an intensity about him that was very, very painful for him.

Put another way, Mark felt emotional pain more deeply than many are able (or willing) to feel it. He was, by his own admission, an emotional man with "out of place feelings" and "obsolete tears."

Unfortunately, places like the church where we learn to care the most for people are also places where we get hurt the most deeply. Echoing Pat's thoughts, Tom Howard commented: "I think given any standard American congregation there was probably just the chance, time and again, [to get deeply hurt] . . . I think [Mark], through his own sense of survival, bowed out of the whole system. But he had a huge heart for God. A huge heart for people."

The hurt Mark felt wasn't merely personal hurt, but hurt for what was being done to the image of Christ. In other words, the same personality issues that caused him to rebel during interviews, or during sappy moments of self-conscious prayer before concerts, were also at work in his relationship to churches. As Dan Russell simply put it, "He couldn't survive the subculture." It was as if he could handle a certain amount of inauthenticity in life at large—the world around him was full of it—but he couldn't take it *within* the church. His view of God was too big, and he knew the church was the one place where people should be authentic and real. Trying to explain Mark's thinking, John Flynn phrased it as such: "[Why] go to church if the trappings make you more frustrated and angry and just totally sidetrack you from the purpose of going there in the first place?"

"I would imagine," Randy Stonehill agreed, "it was partly his private nature and partly [that] his b.s. meter was really sensitive. He knew [that if he went to church] he would want to stand up frequently and [say something like] 'Oh, just stop it! You guys putting your hands up. Don't do that just to look like the other people! You're really bothering me!'" And so it was safer not to go at all.

FOR THE ROCK OF FORGIVENESS TO MELT IN THE RAIN

For several years after Mark Heard's death, I was involved in an online chat group[50] whose nominal purpose was to discuss Mark's music, though conversations as often as not went far afield from that stated topic. The issue of Mark's faith arose from time to time, as people tried to make sense of his songwriting. It was noted that in Mark's later music, there were no blatant simple expressions of Christian faith—or at least not phrased in recognizable language of the christian subculture. As a result, on more than one occasion, participants suggested that Mark had rejected God altogether in his later years. After all, he didn't go to church! (It was never clear to me whether these claims came from fans who had themselves rejected God and wanted to claim Mark as a hero, or from church-goers who wanted to vilify him.)

Of course these types of speculations began long before Mark's death. In the spring of 1986, after the first of his concerts that I ever helped produce, one of my friends complained, "Why didn't he sing about God?" To which another of my friends—one who had been listening more closely—responded, "Why weren't you listening to his songs?" His songs *had* messages steeped in a Christian worldview, with profound insights into both human sinfulness and Divine grace. They just happened to be communicated without the language of the christian subculture.

In a letter to me written on October 27, 1986, Mark shared a few of his insights into the relationship between art and faith. Part of his comments were in response to a quote by C. S. Lewis which I had shared with him[51]:

> If we just create, I don't think our beliefs can help but affect and/or be reflected by the outcome. But I don't think I can sit here and state the absolute purpose of every creative endeavor . . . the ongoing (perhaps lifelong) process of *learning* what art and expression are takes us through mazes we could never comprehend from the vantage point of tenets.

The only observations I might offer would be:

(1) I think we can trust that God will help direct our efforts, maintaining our individuality, even though that help may seem intangible.

(2) That we have the responsibility to go beyond repetition of the attitudes that have given Christianity bad press in society, and to go out of our way to exhibit our own escape from constrictions of both society and Christian society in favor of being *true* in our observations, our attitudes, and our humanity.

These are only observations, and have seemingly little to do with what actually occurs each time we sit down to a blank sheet of paper; the more we do it, the easier it gets, and the more difficult it gets. That enough paradox for you???

In any case—whatever one makes of his songwriting aside—everybody who knew Mark well scoffed at any rumors of a denial of his Christian faith. As Tom Howard explained, with respect to Mark's feelings toward the church as a political institution:

[It was] not a rejection of God at all. In fact, [it was] probably a deepening of his philosophical mind. He loved to sit and talk about Aristotelian philosophy and the difference between that and Platonism. All of the philosophical studies he did—I don't know if they were very in-depth—but they certainly informed his grasp of where he was with his faith.

As Janet came to understand, although Mark was not at all interested in church as a political institution, he was very interested in Church as a body of believers. "If church was with a big 'C,' he'd do it. He had a community of believers, people with whom he worked."

Nevertheless, his stance was a conundrum to many. When Mark died, one thought burned in the minds of some of his friends: "My God, what a talent and heart and gift he would have brought to some congregation." But during Mark's life, that was a thought that remained largely unspoken even among his closest friends, like in a bad marriage where sooner or later there are certain subjects you just don't approach. In any case, Mark probably would have countered with, "Well I brought that to the church with my music."

Which is to say, his heart for God was there. Certainly it was expressed in his music. There was evidence in his songs that he was painfully aware of his own failings, and thus even more aware of God's grace. In "Look Over Your Shoulder," he wrote: "It takes more than your passion and more than your pain for the rock of forgiveness to melt in the rain."

Perhaps that hope came out more rarely in his final three albums, but it was not less powerful. And for some, that made those expressions all the more potent. Steve Hindalong remembers helping Mark record "Look Over Your Shoulder," and it proved a treasured time for Steve:

> [Mark] invited me to play drums on *Second Hand.* I played on five of the tracks in one day. I was pretty nervous about that because I'm not like a session drummer. I'm just a band drummer. But after I did—after I succeeded in getting all those tracks in one day—these cowboy boots I was wearing became my lucky boots. I wore them for four years after that. I can't play the kick drum unless I'm wearing these boots. Because it was a very good day for me.
>
> I think "Look Over Your Shoulder" is my favorite drum track. Extremely subtle. He wanted me to play it with mallets—hard mallets—which is kind of unusual in a drum set: high hats, snares, cymbals, everything. And he wanted me to play real soft. It didn't sound soft. He was great with compressors and so forth. But really, it's just my favorite . . . I think a great song, a great lyric, is great for everybody involved, but for some reason I really love that drum track.

Still, it was hard even for Mark's mother Jean to understand him. After Mark's death, she would often talk to Randy Stonehill on the phone and express her confusion. I think Randy's response to her captures something central about Mark.

> "Well, Jean," he would reply, "he was a man of extraordinary depth. I don't know quite how to describe it, but he just didn't say things in your kind of typical, pat, pop format."
>
> "Yeah," she'd agree. Then the mother in her would come out. "But when I listen to his songs sometimes I would just get so worried. He would just seem so unhappy, you know?"
>
> "Oh Jean, but he loved God and that's why he couldn't turn his eyes from the struggle and the darkness. But you know that

was just because he was an honest man. He had the faith and the courage to look at that stuff. And just when you thought, maybe this guy was just in love with his own depression, that was when he would drop in the kernel of hope and light. He would anchor down his song with the fundamental truth: if there's anything at all in existence to cling to, it is the reality of God's love for us and the hope that comes from the cross. And then, when he talks about the essence of truth, and what the reason for hope is, then it has potency and power! And it pierces you and it jars you and speaks to you because it's not this cheapened little trite phrase that you heard at the end of every verse of some christian pop song, you know?"

THE FALLOUT OF OUR FINGERPRINTS

Though it was a very painful time for Mark, one thing that did come about in the late 1980s, after Mark's parting from Home Sweet Home and the quick demise of WHAT? Records, was the formation of the Fingerprint label. Fingerprint didn't happen overnight, of course. There was a gap of about three years during which time Mark had no label and no contract. In his considerable discouragement during this especially dark period, he told several people (including me) that he'd given up on recording his own music—that he had made his final album. In keeping with that, he did very little touring on his own. His time was mostly spent engineering and producing albums for other people in order to make ends meet.

However he continued to write songs. He also did one extended tour through the United States as a "side man" for Sam Phillips. Dan Russell was with them, working for Principle Management as Sam's manager. "There were about sixty performances on that tour," Dan recalls. Traveling by train, which was Sam's preferred mode of transportation, they had a lot of hours together on the road and got to know each other a lot better.

> There were many, many long nights, sunrises, out-loud dreaming, singing and dancing; lots of bars, clubs, dim rooms . . . early morning cab rides to make the only train out of town, etc. . . . Mark stood in a dim lit shadow, a few feet behind and to the right. He underplayed Sam's wonderful songs. You didn't see his face, but the taste of his playing was distinct, and every night people would comment on Sam's "side" man.

Eventually, Mark got the break he was looking for, and it came in part via the generosity of his old friend Chuck Long. Since the two had first become friends fifteen years earlier, Chuck had gone from working in steel construction to being an anesthesiologist (with several years of school in between). For the first time in his life, Chuck actually had some spare money to spend. Being a musician himself, and having a long-standing love and appreciation for art and music, he offered to help fund the cost of sending Mark back to the studio to record a new album.

When I first met Chuck and offered him my deepest thanks for making Mark's final three albums possible, he laughed a little and said the offer was partly selfish: he loved Mark's music as much as any of us, and after three years of no new albums was dismayed by the thought that Mark might not ever record again. He figured the only way he'd get to hear more was to pay for it to happen. When he made the offer, however, he was thinking of it entirely as a gift. Mark, however, turned around with a counter-proposal: rather than taking the money outright, he suggested that they form a record company together, and Chuck would get to be part owner.

Dan Russell, who became the third partner in this venture, spoke of this time in our interview:

> Fingerprint was mutually born by myself, Chuck, and Mark
> . . . We wanted to find our own "fingerprint." This stood for that
> part of each of us that was bold and unique and brave enough
> to live in the light of day regardless of the reviews, the elders, the
> fans, the lords of the labels, etc. It was absolutely vital to find
> ourselves, be true and encourage anyone we worked with to
> do the same. We believed this path was the only path we could
> survive on.

In some sense, therefore, Fingerprint became a working out of what Mark had written to me in his letter a few years earlier: "We have the responsibility to go . . . out of our way to exhibit our own escape from constrictions of both society and Christian society in favor of being *true* in our observations, our attitudes, and our humanity."

Fortunately, both for Mark and for those looking for the type of music he was writing, there was also a practical side. As Dan explains:

> Fingerprint was created first to provide an outlet, however
> humble, for Mark's music. It was our intention to release demos

that he was recording to finance the month-to-month living allowance. Mark would write and record, and Chuck and I would lend our views, and I would shop his songs in five song demos to every label head and A & R person that made sense.

In other words, Mark's songwriting was the focal point of Fingerprint, Dan Russell was to provide the industry contacts and labor, and Chuck the financial backing. Mark needed this practical help. As Pat Terry commented, "In all the different periods of his life he always had goals and things he wanted to accomplish, but he was uncomfortable with self-promotion. He always looked for and appreciated people who could do those sorts of things."

Of equal or greater importance, Dan and Chuck would also both provide creative feedback as well as emotional, artistic, and spiritual support for Mark. And during the next three years, Mark did indeed call Dan and Chuck frequently—sometimes several days a week—for advice and for opinions on his work. Certainly he needed the encouragement as much as Dan's promotional help. According to Dan, even with Chuck's financial backing, Mark had been burned enough in the past that he was hesitant to go into the studio again. To get the first Fingerprint record made, Dan essentially put Mark's band together for him and almost forced him into a studio. He set up a little rehearsal studio in his barn, got together some very talented musicians (including Fergus Marsh, the Chapman stick player for Bruce Cockburn), and then invited Mark to come out to New England to perform some of his new material. After several days rehearsing in the barn followed by a concert, Dan booked studio time.

The result of this was Mark's first album in several years: *Dry Bones Dance*, which featured, along with Mark and Fergus: David Birmingham on drums, Byron Berline on fiddle and mandolin, and an appearance by Michael Been of The Call. Without the distribution of any major label, the album sold more than 15,000 copies. Over the next two years, Mark would go on to record two more albums with Fingerprint, *Second Hand* and *Satellite Sky*, and the label would also sign Bill Mallonee's *Vigilantes of Love*.

THE GODS OF THE HUNT

1987, previously unreleased

The velvet of the evening hills in charcoal silhouette

Soft to the touch of a thousand watching eyes

Twilight star burns cold blue, it burns cold blue

In the hot blue of a thousand dying skies

Another working day in the cinderblock savannah

Weary braves home from the hunt

Another night sleepless beneath skins of prize prey

Another lampful of oil burnt

> Light the fire
>
> Dance to the gods of the hunt

A dim dawn filters down through steely stalagmites

Safe from the heat

Safe from the fire of the stars

Sleepless dreamers move in yellow chariots

And speed to meet the warriors

The warriors of the revolving doors

Spearheads and scimitars in corporate tribunal

Someone must fall to the sword

Steam rise from warm blood in cold air of midtown

That's what these weapons are for

> Light the fire
>
> Dance to the gods of the hunt
>
>> We struggle to become the victims of fortune

We grapple to be what no man should want to be

We struggle to become the victims of fortune

We labor to learn of the weakness of strength

Light the fire

Light the fire

Dance to the gods of the hunt

Light the fire

Dance to the gods of the hunt

THIS IS YOUR CHANCE
1987, previously unreleased

You have got the touch of the falling snow

You have got a kiss like a sonic boom

You are like a wave with an undertow

But (darling) when you break you're just a shallow pool

Baby baby don't you think there is more to you and me

Don't you think a true-blue friend could be what the both of us need

 This is your chance to show me what you know about love

 This is your chance to show me what you know about love

You have got a face from the renaissance

You have got a heart like a violin

Looking for a classical counterpoint

There is more to music than an instrument

Baby baby don't you think there's something that you've overlooked

Don't you think a true-blue friend can't be caught with hints or with hooks

This is your chance to show me what you know about love

This is your chance to show me what you know about love

You would like to lasso a shooting star

Like to ride a barrel in a waterfall

You'll be anybody but who you are

Cinderella waiting for the prince to call

Baby baby don't you think there is more to you and me

Don't you think a true-blue friend is really what the both of us need

   This is your chance to show me what you know about love

   This is your chance to show me what you know about love

MYSTERY MIND

1988, previously unreleased

"I need you" was all I said

But she did not hear a word

Something else was what she heard

Was it something I said

"What I meant was I love you"

"I just can't" was her reply

And the rain fell from her eyes

While she stared at her shoes

If I could get her to give me a clue to her mystery mind

She might feel that she could be better

She might feel that she could just go on and

Stare straight at me with her serious eyes

I said "Please I hate to pry"

"Well then don't" she told my eyes

Mumbling something about some child

Born to troublesome times

She has quite a handsome smile

But it fades

And she can look like she's been riding on the back of a tiger

Through a tunnel of fire

If I could get her to give me a clue to her mystery mind

She might feel that she could be better

She might feel that she could just go on and

Stare straight at me with her serious eyes

I have heard that love is blind

But I see her all too well

How she keeps things to herself

Like she's the scene of a crime

Will I go down to my grave

Never having known her touch

Never managing so much as to hold her in vain

If I could get her to give me a clue to her mystery mind

She might feel that she could be better

She might feel that she could just go on and

Stare straight at me with her serious eyes

WAITING FOR DRY BONES TO DANCE

1988, previously unreleased

What remains of a love poem
Long after the ink is dry
Yellowed paper and silent mouths
A bit of skeletal passion
Bleached relics of wasted youth
Hanging on like desert flowers

I am alone and I'm
Waiting for dry bones, waiting for dry bones
Waiting for dry bones to dance

Read the wisdom of our lovers
Catechism of spark and fire
By the light of the burning bridge
True fossil of affection
True rock in the sediment
Dry river expose your veins

I am alone and I'm
Waiting for dry bones, waiting for dry bones
Waiting for dry bones to dance

Bring the wind to the city
Let it weep in the empty streets
At the tomb of the unknown race
Skyscrapers and windmills
White crosses and pyramids
Every hand tries to leave some trace

I am alone and I'm
Waiting for dry bones, waiting for dry bones
Waiting for dry bones to dance

NEVER AND ALWAYS

1988, previously unreleased

You never aim to please

You always miss the mark

Never and always

Never and always

I never shoot to kill

But I always hit your heart

Never and always

Never and always

 I can never seem to reach you—sometimes

 I am always here to speak to you—sometimes, sometimes

I never speak my mind

But you're always getting hurt

Never and always

Never and always

You never hold it back

But you always waste your words

Never and always

Never and always

 I can never seem to please you—sometimes

 I am always here to hear you—sometimes, sometimes

We never mean to fail

We always fail to touch

LOOKING FOR A GOOD TIME

1987, previously unreleased

Taking his cue from the fool on the hill he moves uptown

Living it up like a lonely man will—he'll be back down

Shaking the dust from his traveling clothes under the lights

Leaving his senses to follow his nose into the night

Oooooooh Looking for a good time

Holding her head like an angel of light

She's Helen of Troy

Or one of those things on the bow of a ship

Luck for the boys

She hangs around at the officers' club breaking their hearts

Leaves around ten when she's tired of the bluff

And bored with the farce

Checking his suit like he's going to church

He pulls on his shoes

Looks out the window

And squints at the earth's changing tattoos

He thinks of emotions to which he's immune

Sweat on his hands

He opens the hatch and steps down on the moon

Small step for man

{7}

TREASURE OF THE BROKEN LAND

"It's always hard to lose a friend, the separation that death brings is

a reality that I don't like to face. A phone call won't do anymore. But what I do have

are the memories, the times we recorded music together, the time we spent in Europe

together, and all the jokes that Mark would tell over and over and over again. And

Mark's music, all of the songs that continue to make me feel, every time I hear them.

Mark's friendship and music touched my life deeply, and I am forever grateful."

—Derri Daugherty[52]

"I hope it's true that God takes the best the earliest so that they don't

have to endure the garbage for the whole long run. I almost felt like Mark's life was

so intense; it's almost like he lived it in half the time a normal person would. And his

contribution was so rich. Perhaps God said, 'Alright, you've done well. You don't have

to go the distance. You can come home.'"

—Randy Stonehill[53]

TREASURE OF THE BROKEN LAND

1992, *Satellite Sky*

I see you now and then in dreams

Your voice sounds just like it used to

I know you better than I knew you then

All I can say is I love you

I thought our days were commonplace

Thought they would number in millions

Now there's only the aftertaste of circumstance

that can't pass this way again

Treasure of the broken land

Parched earth give up your captive ones

Waiting wind of Gabriel

Blow soon upon the hollow bones

I saw the city at its tortured worst

And you were outside the walls there

You were relieved of a lifelong thirst

I was dry at the fountain

I knew that you could see my shame

But you were eyeless and sparing

I awoke when you called my name

I felt the curtain tearing

Treasure of the broken land

Parched earth give up your captive ones

Waiting wind of Gabriel

Blow soon upon the hollow bones

I can melt the clock hands down

But only in my memory

Nobody gets the second chance to be the friend they meant to be

I see you now and then in dreams

Your voice sounds just like it used to

I believe I will hear it again

God how I love you

Treasure of the broken land

Parched earth give up your captive ones

Waiting wind of Gabriel

Blow soon upon the hollow bones

NOW AND THEN IN DREAMS

Who was Mark Heard? If nothing else, the writing of this book has made me realize how complex he really was. There were no simple answers—no single summary statements that would do justice to him as a person. "He was funny," Pierce Pettis wrote. "A curmudgeon. Brilliant. Fun. Hot tempered. Forgiving. Humble. Honest. He was the single funniest person I ever met—and one of the most sincere."

Dan Russell wrote:

> Mark was a dear friend, a brother, a poet, a musician, an engineer, a producer, a songwriter, a photographer, a filmmaker, a writer, a painter. But primarily this artist was a broken man who humbly loved his wife and daughter and sought to provide for them the best he could.

"A deep-feeling and sensitive man," Bill Mallonee described him, "but one crushed by his circumstances and who was burning both ends of an invisible candle."

Prisca Sandri, the daughter of Francis Shaeffer's and a long-time friend of Mark, was remembering Mark to his daughter Rebecca. "He was always so preoccupied in getting just the right sound and had such a deep insight into the world and emotions. He was also so funny and would have us all laughing often."[54]

"He was a great storyteller," Randy Stonehill echoes. "A very funny guy. Enormously gifted."

"I got the impression Mark could play anything," Jason Harrod recalled, from the brief time he knew Mark. "He played six or seven instruments on our album, and seemed equally proficient in all of them."

John Austin ended our interview with his own poignant thought.

> Mark hated being rejected, the pain of it, the painful situation it put his family in—but he did his work. He did what he was put on this planet to do, and he did it better than anyone I've ever met. He was his fingerprints. Maybe that sounds trite—but in an age where being human is becoming more difficult, that is victory.

Buddy remembers the last (and only) time he and Mark ever performed together. It was a benefit concert for Victoria Williams, held at The Whiskey in Los Angeles. Buddy, Julie and Mark were driving to town together. They were in Mark's great old Cadillac, because Mark wouldn't ride in anything else; he needed to have lots of steel around him in order to feel safe.

> I remember he was talking about how this heart thing ran in his family. And how he probably wasn't going to live that long. It was pretty morose at the time. [And yet somehow] it was funny—not your ordinary *go-to-the-gig-talk*. We knew how he loved Janet, and how he just loved his daughter [Rebecca] so much. Maybe the nature of the gig had him thinking about that, being real sick.

Unfortunately, the discussion proved prophetic. In July of 1992, less than a year after John Mark Heard Jr. died, John Mark Heard III succumbed himself to the heart disease that ran in his family. Mark suffered a heart attack in the middle of a song, during a concert at the famed Cornerstone Festival. Amazingly, he managed to finish the song before walking off stage. Pierce Pettis and Kate Miner (then known as Pam Dwinell-Miner) were on stage with Mark at the time of his heart attack. Recalls Pierce:

> I remember he did an amazing set, came off the stage and just slumped down into a folding chair backstage. The audience was still on their feet, stomping and clapping for an encore. I said to Mark, "Hey, I think they want you to do an encore."

> He said, "you do it."

> It was at that point I noticed how bad he looked, and he was saying he didn't feel right and thought maybe we should get a doctor or something. He was obviously in pain and his color was bad. So we got on the walkie-talkie and called for medical help—which I remember seemed to take a really long time getting there. The next day, I drove down to Springfield, IL to see him in the hospital. Mark was in intensive care, and I was the only other person there besides the nurse. (His family had not arrived from California yet). It was the fourth of July in Lincoln's hometown, and everything seemed very quiet and eerie. Mark and I just talked. I think he was pretty scared that what was happening to him was a repeat of what had happened to his dad just a few months prior . . .

> I tried to reassure him that whatever had happened to his dad need not happen to him, that every case was different.

After that, he seemed to lighten up and I remember we spent a very pleasant time together, just joking and light conversation. Don't remember exactly what we talked about, but I know he appreciated me being there and I was glad I had come. He seemed to be his old self again.

When it started getting late I decided I'd better go on as I had a long drive ahead and knew [his family] would arrive shortly. So I said, "take care, see you later," or words to that effect. That was the last time I saw him. Getting on the elevator to go down, I met Janet and Rebecca, who were just coming up. I knew he was in good hands then.

YOUR VOICE SOUNDS JUST LIKE IT USED TO

Indeed, in all the work of writing this book, the most poignant and moving moments for me were listening to friends recall their final memories of Mark. Their own words speak more loudly than anything I could add. For Randy Stonehill, that last encounter was backstage at a U2 concert in L.A. Randy had just completed *Wonderama*, and Mark had simultaneously been completing *Satellite Sky* and co-producing (with Peter Buck of R.E.M.) the album *Killing Floor* for Bill Mallonee and V.O.L.

I saw him and I said, "Hey Mark, I want to thank you for your input . . . *Wonderama* came out to be a very different record because you inspired me. You sort of kicked my butt and made me go really shake it down and shake things up and try to deliver my best, you know? And, I would really like you to hear it."

And I asked him what he had been doing and he told me. "Well you know, I've been working with Peter Buck [on the V.O.L. album. Also] I did this project . . . of my own called *Satellite Sky*."

So, I said, "Oh man I'd really like to hear it."

And I'll never forget this. This was the last picture in my memory of him. In the dimly-lit backstage area, there he is looking like the wise owl with too much curly hair which is all gone gray now and his round John Lennon glasses, and with his ever-present Camel cigarette smoke kind of wafting out in front of his face like some kind of incense from a prayer or something. And he looked at me, and he said, "Well, c'mon by. I'll be around."

That's the last time I saw him. And the additional irony was . . .
that I didn't hear *Satellite Sky* until after he had died. And then I
sat in my living room listening to this stunning masterpiece, like a
parting gift to the planet. It was almost like a man who knew that
he was gonna be out of here. Because I just thought, "You don't
ever have to do another thing again; this has so much; this is so
dense; it's got such substance, such brilliance . . . It could stand as
your final definitive statement." I couldn't listen to anything but
Mark's music after his death, for months.

One of the albums Mark produced toward the end of his life was Pierce
Pettis' *Tinseltown*. So deeply touched was Pierce by Mark's life and music—
and so frustrated by Mark's lack of recognition—that when Mark died,
Pierce committed himself to covering a Mark Heard song on every album
he recorded after that. "Every day I'm finding out more what he meant to
me," Pierce wrote to me. "I've had other friends pass away, but none has
left an impression on me like Mark has."

Susan Heard had her own sisterly reflections:

> I miss talking to him every week, and also laughing with him.
> Mark could really laugh. He could impersonate almost anyone
> and would have everybody rolling in the aisles with some of his
> renditions . . .

> To me, Mark was such a real person. He had fears and
> moodiness, a lot of which are evident in his songs, and he could
> be difficult to live with, as can we all. However I don't think I
> could have asked for a better brother, and I am very grateful that
> we grew so close in the years before he died—I wouldn't trade the
> relationship I had with him for anything.

When Tom Howard pulls up his most telling memories of Mark, it is
not of the last few months of Mark's life—a time when they had drifted in
different directions and were spending less time together—but the middle
period of their friendship.

> We would be engrossed in dinners and conversations and
> philosophical stuff, talking about a movie we saw, or a book we
> read, and the spiritual application of a Gene Wilder movie or
> something. We were trying to figure it all out back then. And I
> miss the intensity of those conversations. And the fun of them. We

laughed. We laughed our butts off all the time. Something would hit Mark funny and he'd just collapse. I think I heard from Janet that he died laughing, because he was laughing at something that Kate [Miner] had sent him,* and he was laughing his butt off, and that's when he had his second heart attack. I mean, he'd just about have a heart attack when he'd laugh. He'd be wheezing, he'd be laughing so hard. His laugh was infectious.

Not surprisingly, Steve Hindalong's final memory was more painful, and yet still humorous in its way, and also profound. He was still angry at Mark for not being willing to perform on the *At The Foot of the Cross* set. So when Mark did his own set, Steve went instead to hear Adam Again who were playing at the same time. He and a few others were driving home from the gig after midnight when they saw the ambulance and heard a rumor that Mark had suffered some kind of a heart attack. But all Steve could think about was the smoke machine years earlier at the concert in Holland, and how Mark had made such a big deal out of it and passed out on stage. Steve could only laugh. "'They'd got an ambulance picking him up for *that?*' we said. 'What is he doing this time?' We just thought it was some nutty thing."

Then at four in the morning, Pierce Pettis called him and said, "You know, Steve, we've got to go to the hospital."

Steve was incredulous. "Mark is actually at the hospital?"

"This is serious," Pierce replied.

So Steve got up in the early morning hours and went to the hospital. He sat in the lobby for an hour but couldn't see Mark. The whole time he was thinking, "I'm not going to stay in this lobby because Mark was bothered by a smoke machine." He never talked to Mark again. "I never really believed it was true that he was going to die," Steve told me, nine and a half years later. "There never was closure for me."

PARCHED EARTH GIVE UP YOUR CAPTIVE ONES

If the final lasting memories of Mark's life were poignant and telling, the stunned disbelief and reactions to his death were even more so.

"I remember sitting in the motel room in Macon, the night before his funeral," Randy Stonehill told me. "David Edwards . . . and I were sharing a

*Actually it was Mark's sister, see Endnote #1. Ed.

room. I was just sitting there stunned at this sense of loss both personally and just the sense of loss I felt for art, you know, at his early exit."

There were lots of pauses in the conversation as Randy fought to tell me this story over dinner at a small restaurant in Seal Beach.

I remember sitting there looking at Dave and saying, "You know, I always knew that Mark was special." I really did. And I don't think I was romanticizing it. I just knew. I could hear it in his work. I even said to him, "Mark, what do you eat right before you go to sleep that makes you dream up lyrics, what books do you read?"

And he would just kind of laugh and go "Oh, I don't know. I just kind of wander around in my underwear, and I don't know."

He never really talked much about the process. And the guy was so busy just trying to keep the wolf from the door, doing project after project. I thought, "when on earth does this man even have time to write?" But he was so brilliant that he seemed to feel so much and see so much that it just came percolating out of him.

So, I just was sitting there—feeling like I had been kicked in the stomach—sitting there in the motel room with David. I couldn't believe the next day we were going to go this guy's funeral. And with that heightened sense of what we'd lost and his death, I turned to David and I said "David, do you realize? Do you know how good he was?"

And I know David did. He just kind of looked at me, and I said "You know what? He could sit in a room doing songwriter-in-the-round, in a songwriter session with Paul Simon, Joni Mitchell, Bob Dylan, Elvis Costello. Anybody you'd care to name, and he could hold his own. That's how good he was!" And David just nodded in affirmation.

Even Bruce Cockburn, who had only recently started to get to know Mark, was intensely moved:

When Mark died, I wasn't prepared for how deeply it would affect me. I'm not inclined to be sentimental about death. I have a sort of easy-come easy-go attitude, generally speaking. But there was a small group of us that cared very deeply about Mark's presence on the planet. It wasn't a question of his personality . . . It was the fact that he was there doing the quality of work and the kind of songwriting he was doing. And known by so few people. [For] those of us who did know him, it seems like he provided a sort of link among a group of us. And when he died, there was a sort of hole there."[55]

BLOW SOON UPON THESE HOLLOW BONES

For Randy, the memories have intensified over the years.

I still think about him almost every night backstage before I go on. I think about stuff he said to me. "Randy, just be yourself, let the song tell the story. Remember why you wrote the song! And it'll speak." And then he'd say funny things like "This is just the weirdest kind of work in the world, isn't it, because you have to concentrate 1000%, but hey, don't tense up!"

And, I think about his life; I think about the integrity of his approach to a performance and to an audience. Every night of my career before I walk out on stage . . . to this day, that remains a compass that helps guide me into doing some kind of a meaningful, honest performance.

It is in these memories, perhaps, that we understand both what Mark gave us and also how great the tragedy of his loss really was. He was at once both surprisingly simple and incomprehensibly complex: caring, generous, and sweetly sentimental, but also stubborn and abrupt. He could write some of the most profound lyrics of his generation one minute, and get absorbed in an episode of *Gilligan's Island* the next. He was an emotional man, and a broken man. To borrow Frederick Buechner's imagery once again, Mark's faith clung to him like a torn and tattered trench coat.

Sitting on a park bench just outside of Nashville, I listened to Tom Howard summarize this as well as I've heard anybody put it to words.

What I miss most about Mark is the potential that was there— of course in his art and music—but also in long-term friendships. I miss what could have been between him and me. I think we had stretches of time where we didn't connect hardly at all, and then a project would bring us together.

I miss—like you would with any friend that is gone—what could have been. You long for the end of the story. And the end of the story went away. For Mark, and for everybody who loved him and knew him, the story was snipped out right at mid-book. And that was the tragedy of it.

I miss Rebecca having known her dad, having grown up with her dad. His mother living out her years without a grown son.

I miss the good times. I miss the conversations. Like everybody else who knew him. But I miss the future. Mark and I hadn't had a lot of contact for a couple of years really—and when he first had the heart attack I got a hold of him. We had a laugh. He seemed in good spirits. And then I never talked to him again.

Yet somehow there was a sense of completeness to it all. The story was snipped out mid-book, as Tom said, but Tom also witnessed a certain closure. Ultimately, it revolved around relationship.

It's very interesting. You can look at it as bookends. When I first met Mark, he was there with Chuck Long. They were at my house yukking it up. So on and so forth. That was the first meeting.

[And then after his death] I decided I really wanted to say goodbye to Mark personally. So I flew out to Macon for his funeral, and I played piano at his funeral at his mom's request. I had a strange detachment from the whole thing. I didn't know what to feel. I didn't know where to put anything. I felt like our friendship had drifted off a little. But I wanted to be there. I wanted to be in Macon. I was fishing for what my emotions were, because it was all so fresh. Just like everybody else's were. Because Mark was such a paradox. Such an enigma. The people that were closest to him had a lot of sorting out to do when he checked out.

Well anyway, I was standing at his gravesite with the coffin—the closed casket. I was standing there quietly, and Chuck Long walked over to the casket, and put his hand on it, and started crying. And I lost it. That was the arc. When I met Mark he was with Chuck, and when I said goodbye to Mark, there he was with his best friend Chuck Long. It was the arc of my knowing Mark. There he was with his good friend. And there he was at the end of his life again. I just observed it. I was always the observer with those guys. I'd get the biggest kick out of them. Just listening to them. They would cut up all the time. I was the audience. I was their crowd, which I felt happy to be. They never made me feel excluded. They had their thing. And there I was standing at this gravesite and there was Chuck again.

I HANG MY HEAD

1987, previously unreleased

Wish that I had seen it before

She was worth much more than I planned

Now I stand elected as fool of the month

Just a taste of love can kill you

Like shallow breathing underwater

I know that hearts can be accident-prone

I hang my head

I've got three little words

I hang my head

They will never be heard

I had better lose her number

I can't recall it at the moment

Torment—I told her I loved her too late

Checking my reaction to pain

I have had a change of address

Yes I'm living in heartbreak hotel

I hang my head

I've got three little words

I hang my head

They will never be heard

How could I have been so stupid

And where was Cupid with his arrows

Sorrow, come have a drink with your lad

I laughed with her like with a sister

While I contemplated love's cost
I lost the best friend that I ever had

I hang my head
I've got three little words
I hang my head
They will never be heard

WHEN HIS LUCK RUNS OUT

1989, previously unreleased

He is a lucky man

He's got things

He's got two of anything you could name

Two Cadillacs

Two homes

Too many friends

He is never alone

If there's one thing a lucky man don't need

It's a doubt

Just one step away from being down and out

Where's he gonna be when his luck runs out

WHEN HIS LUCK RUNS OUT

WHEN HIS LUCK RUNS OUT

WHEN HIS LUCK RUNS OUT

WHEN HIS LUCK RUNS, LUCK RUNS, LUCK RUNS OUT

He buys caviar

He buys wine

He buys Japanese businessmen's time

Black cigarettes

Rolled up in France

A skosh of extra room

In the seat of his pants

When he throws a party

Well you better come out

Listen to everybody wonder

While he sings and shouts

Where's he gonna be when his luck runs out

WHEN HIS LUCK RUNS OUT

WHEN HIS LUCK RUNS OUT

WHEN HIS LUCK RUNS OUT

WHEN HIS LUCK RUNS, LUCK RUNS, LUCK RUNS OUT

Lady luck, she's a top-notch babe

She give and give

Til you got it made

Like I said, she's a hot-shot

She got what it takes

To take what you've got

She's a religion and the man is devout

But she can leave him praying in the poor house

Where's he gonna be when his luck runs out

WHEN HIS LUCK RUNS OUT

WHEN HIS LUCK RUNS OUT

WHEN HIS LUCK RUNS OUT

WHEN HIS LUCK RUNS, LUCK RUNS, LUCK RUNS OUT

SEASON OF WORDS

1989, previously unreleased

Neon lights up on this roof

Never get brighter and never go off

Just like me and just like you

Average people with the average blues

How did it come to this

What kind of coverage did we give to ourselves

So we wouldn't be lonely

A SEASON OF WORDS

A SEASON OF TEARS

A HALL OF MIRRORS IN A SEASON OF FEARS

SHADOWS ON YOU

SHADOWS ON ME

SHADOWS ON THE PEOPLE WE WERE MEANT TO BE

We might look and we might pry

With the eyes of a child

But we are not children

Children play and children cry

Simple things summon the tears to their eyes

We might've been so young

But for the constant drone

That's making us old

The usual distractions

A SEASON OF WORDS

A SEASON OF TEARS

A HALL OF MIRRORS IN A SEASON OF FEARS

SHADOWS ON YOU

SHADOWS ON ME

SHADOWS ON THE PEOPLE WE WERE MEANT TO BE

Nothing is moving tonight

Only the weeds that grow

In the cracks of the asphalt

Under the streetlights

Souls will come and souls will go

And trying to get ourselves used to the flow

We say goodbye

And say hello

And anything else that might help us to cope

I might've felt the rain

I might've seen the sun

But the curtains are drawn

And it's safe to be lonely

[CHORUS]

[Janet and Rebecca, Christmas 2001.]

[AFTERWORD]

At first it was hard to read this book—too many memories. It hurt as I recalled Mark's inner turmoil, his struggle to be different than most because he was. He truly expected people to see things as deeply as he did. Mark had such strong convictions. He wanted to follow God's will for his life. He loved music. Could God actually want him to do something he loved? As he recorded albums and people responded and identified with the lyrics and music, he slowly came to believe that it was okay. He desperately wanted to support me and Rebecca with the music he wrote and the projects he produced. And he did! As I read the book again, though, I found myself thinking how well friends portrayed Mark. He was a great storyteller, loved to laugh, felt things passionately. He thrived when he was in the studio working on one of his own albums or someone else's. I am grateful to Matt and everyone who contributed to this book. Between Mark's music and this book, Rebecca is learning more about the father she never got a chance to know. Ten years have passed and we still live in the same house. Rebecca has started high school. She loves music and after playing trumpet, clarinet, and piano, she is now taking guitar lessons. We talk frequently of ways she is like her dad. I work full time for a medical publishing company where I have been for sixteen years. We are grateful for our family and friends who add so much to our lives. Thank you, Matt, for putting so much time and care into this project and for having the idea of interviewing friends and family who could paint a fuller picture of Mark's life. Thanks to Cornerstone Press for acting on their interest in having his story told. My thanks too to everyone who listened and continues to listen to Mark's music. I hope it speaks to you on many levels and touches your soul. I hope it makes a difference in your life. It has—and does—in mine.

—Janet Heard

{APPENDIX 1}

LIFE IN THE INDUSTRY: A MUSICIAN'S DIARY
BY MARK HEARD

Originally appeared in *Image:*
A Journal of the Arts and Religion, **2** (1992)

INTRODUCTION

I much prefer making music to talking about it. There's something visceral about instruments and voices that transcends words. Louis Armstrong once told somebody, "If you have to ask what jazz is, you'll never know," or something like that.

I'm drawn to producing because it is intuitive. I try to figure out who the artist really and truly is musically, and then capture that on a tape recorder. In this day and age, it is becoming increasingly difficult to concentrate on this, because of the nature of the multi-track recording process itself and because of the double-duty a producer must do, assisting the artist and answering to the record company for the commercial values of creative choices.

I have had some production contracts with clauses that stipulate the final product must be both technically and commercially acceptable, with the producer held liable should it fail to do so. Of course, luckily, the persons to whom I was contracted happened to be human beings and to love music, and we talked on the phone a lot, and Fed Exed rough mixes back and forth so this was not really a problem, but I can imagine that out there in the big-time world it might not be nice to have to be a producer sometimes.

Technology has made it possible for recordings to be as near perfect as possible. You can have an artist spend hours or days on one vocal, filling up countless tracks with alternate takes and assembling the best of all the syllables together, or "punching in" a line until it is perfect. This is such a common practice that our ears have become accustomed to it, and to be competitive, one must always bear in mind those who spend many hours and many dollars to get the perfect take. It's common for records to cost hundreds of thousands of dollars to make, and for hundreds of hours of studio time to be expended.

I find myself increasingly drawn to the older spontaneous approach. In the early days, things were taken down live, as they happened, in their entirety. Of course, there could be more than one take to choose from, but when music was mixed directly or mono, there was an energy that is difficult to capture today. I've seen films of Tony Bennett singing live with an orchestra from sheet music and emoting like crazy, and getting it in one take.

George Harrison said of the early Beatles' recordings, "The first album took eight hours to record—the second one even longer."

I like to get an artist ready to do his vocals, get him to remember why he wrote the song, and then get him to sing it without pretension and without melodrama. I always keep the first take, even if there are flat notes, and I generally will not let an artist keep singing past four or five takes. I like to use one take all the way through the song, if possible. Competitively speaking, there will always be many subtle sharps, flats and rough edges, and by market standards the records I make won't sound as commercial because of this, but I have come to believe that it is these flaws that make a track believable. Luckily, I have worked with some gifted artists, who are accustomed to performing their material solo. The hardest thing is figuring out what else to add once the basic instruments and vocal are on tape.

Each song dictates a mood of sorts, sometimes from the outset, and sometimes as it grows, and I try to follow intuition and look for sounds and instruments that reinforce that mood. That is the part I love the most. If it means in a quiet song turning up a Vox amplifier to full volume and playing a distorted harmonic, I can put several different echoes on it and pull the fader way back in the mix, and it will just be a color. Sounds are indeed like colors, and my hunger for a truer palette of colors grows day to day.

In one song, nothing but a Digeridoo would do. It took me several days to track down somebody who could play one, and he said the only note it played was a G sharp, and the song was in G. Luckily, we could varispeed the tape recorder and have his texture. Making an album should be fun and not clinical, I think. I am apt to hire musicians sometimes because I know they will have some good jokes to tell. There is nothing like a good joke, usually in the company of musicians I know, the dirtier, the better, to take an artist's mind off: Oh-my-God, this-is-going-on-tape-and-I'm-going-to-have-to-live-with-it-forever-and-ever. It is usually the human things I remember from my sessions rather than the technicalities. I rarely use charts, indeed, I don't read music, and some of my favorite players are the ones who see the session as a jam. I'll never forget Byron Berline coming over to play fiddle on Garth Hewitt's record the day after Scuds began landing in Israel. Garth's song was a waltz and began, "Ten measures of sorrow God gave to the world, nine to Jerusalem, one to the rest." It was inspired by Garth's visit with some Melchite friends in East Jerusalem, and had given him a real feeling for the sadness of the situation of the Palestinians living there.

I was setting up a headphone mix for Byron as I played the tape, and he didn't even ask the key or anything, but began playing from the top, without a complete cue mix. Of course, I had hit the record button just in case, and he nailed the whole song first take without ever having heard it before. He was playing his heart out.

I told him it was a keeper, and he, much impressed with the timeliness of the song, asked Garth, "Did you write that song last night?" His emotion about the war was part and parcel of his performance, as it was a jam to him. That's what music is about, and those are the types of experiences I value most in looking for the visceral and unidentifiable thing it is that makes music music, and not something else.

THE RADIO–APRIL, 1990

For the past month I have been producing a Christian artist. The record company is concerned about his sales figures, and would like to boost them by having some songs which would be considered as singles for Christian radio. I have to keep reminding myself that this is normal in an economy such as ours.

The big rock stations have to be careful in selecting their playlists to get the maximum number of listeners, in order to be able to charge the maximum amount for advertising time on their stations. There are even organizations that test market songs long before they ever get to the airplay stage so that the choices from which playlists are made are as riskless as possible.

The Christian stations operate under similar principles. Every station manager must worry that if enough people call to complain about a song and nothing is done, Joe's Tire Store down the street might pull its advertising. That's a fact of life. You have to play it safe if your livelihood depends on not offending anyone to this extent.

Obviously, this stifles the creative output of aspiring artists—this imperative to fit the mold. Those who refuse suffer financially—which is also the kiss of death in a capitalist society that knows the price of everything and the value of so little.

The radio guy at the Christian record company called the artist and me to a meeting, where he discussed his strategy for breaking this artist on Christian radio.

First, he suggested some things we not do. On the artist's previous album, which I had produced, we had used some standup bass, fiddle and pedal steel. Our radio man explained to us that these were no-no's this time around. He said the radio stations were scared to play anything with those instruments in them, that it sounded too ethnic. I replied that we had already planned to use standup bass on the new album, and he said, "Well, if you must, but just have the guy play the roots—none of those high-slidey types of notes—nothing too 'ethnic.'"

He proceeded to play us a few songs that were making it on Christian radio. Surprisingly, they were not necessarily heavy in theology—in fact quite the contrary. The lyrics were safe and warm and positive with a bit of mild social concern thrown in now and then. The instrumentation was primarily synthesizer oriented. Very shimmery sounds. Very cut upbeat tempos. Reminded me of the Osmonds.

I got angry. I'm not sure at whom. We began the sessions for the basic tracks of drums and the artist's acoustic guitar. We worked for several days on this, getting a number of songs done, but something in me wanted to play devil's advocate and make a really big hit for Christian radio. I asked the artist if he didn't have some other songs he'd never played me, perhaps something he considered really stupid and inane. It turned out he had just such a chorus. While the drummer had coffee, the artist and I quickly wrote a couple of verses and a bridge, and the song was ready to record. The drummer was playing too good, I felt. I told him to play stupider fills, like "the people" want to hear. It was a really sappy track.

Next day I called in a keyboardist and asked him to play me his three most "Christian" patches. One of them was bell-piano-shimmery-ish, and I said, "Perfect." Although he is an accomplished player, I had him lay down a simple track full of sweet major thirds. Next came the percussionist. I asked him to not bring his great collection of Latin and African fare, but the cutest instruments he had, like bell trees, sleigh bells, claves, little bongos, shakers and the like. I had him play warm and fuzzy little counter-hooks through the song—things that might seem like real production value to people who might not know better.

The background vocalists, who normally do more rock stuff, got into the silly mood with me and came up with some really sappy parts, like something out of a bad lounge act in the seventies. The bass player did big, solid roots, with the occasional pickup as stylized by LA session bassists in the early seventies.

Everything was finally on the tape. The dictum of, "No—play something even stupider" had paid off. I made a mix with the drums way back (loud drums are a no-no on Christian radio unless you are a very big star—so I put all the drums on one sub-fader for the record company guy to handle himself—where they ended up was 15dB down [I measured it with an oscillator] from where I had them.

I turned my mix of this new song from the "No, Play Stupider" sessions in. The next day I got a phone call from the radio guy who was very excited. His actual words were, "Mark, we had no idea you were capable of such brilliant production work." I wished I had videotaped the sessions. when the song was released, it went to number two on Nationwide Christian radio, and stayed on the chart a good while. Everybody at the record company was excited. After all, these are the sorts of things that assure they'll be able to keep making their car payments and buying shoes for their kids.

I understand that—it's just a job. But I'm not sure how I'm supposed to feel. The whole process had nothing to do with Christianity or excellence; only with making something that sounds like something else you've heard a million times before, and will hear a million times again.

We were recording a song called "I Don't Ever Want To Be Without You." The same Christian record company radio guy called me and asked me if we could change the song's title and lyrics. When I asked why, he said, "Because there are two negative words in the title—don't and without . . . I'd like some positive ones; can you call the song, 'I Always Want To Be With You?'"

I have had similar experiences on several occasions with my own songs. It's terribly demeaning to write something that tells its story in its own way and be told it fails because it might scare somebody. My God, must we speak with all the candor of a wax Elvis?

Fergus Marsh, a stick player from Canada, and I were working together recently and talking about my experiences with Christian radio, and he mentioned that his brother, Hugh, had recorded an album with a song called, "Rules Were Made To Be Broken," which was constructed of excerpts from a book called *The Bass Saxophone* by a fellow named Joseph Skvorecky.

I got a copy and couldn't believe how frighteningly similar to my experience were some of the rules binding dance orchestras in Nazi Germany—for violation of which a number of musicians were imprisoned in death camps. I quote:

> In this so-called jazz type repertoire, preference is to be given to compositions in a major key and to lyrics expressing joy in life rather than Jewishly gloomy lyrics; as to tempo, preference is also to be given to brisk compositions over slow ones; however, the pace must not exceed a certain degree of allegro commensurate with the Aryan sense of discipline and moderation. On no account will Negroid excesses in tempo be tolerated.
>
> So-called jazz compositions may contain at most 10% syncopation; the remainder must consist of a natural legato movement devoid of the hysterical rhythmic reverses characteristic of the music of the barbarian races and conducive to dark instincts alien to the German people. Strictly prohibited is the use of instruments alien to the German spirit, as well as all mutes which turn the noble sound of wind and brass instruments into a Jewish-Free-Masonic yowl. Also prohibited are so-called drum breaks longer than half a bar in four-quarter beat (except in stylized military marches); the double bass must be played solely with the bow in so-called jazz compositions; if a pizzicato effect is absolutely desirable for the character of the composition, strict care must be taken lest the string be allowed to patter on the fingerboard which is henceforth strictly forbidden.
>
> All light orchestras and dance bands are advised to restrict the use of saxophones and substitute for them a suitable folk instrument.

Nothing too ethnic y'all, none of them slidey-type notes.

Heil, baby. Yessir, boss.

POLITICS

Today I had an interview with an executive from a Christian record company who was interested in signing me to a recording contract. We met for lunch in North Hollywood in one of those trendy Italian vegetarian places where there are six or seven different types of mineral water on the menu.

Allowances were made for each party to give his life story in five minutes or less, between bites of garlic bread and shallots, despite interruptions from the waitress who would be leaving for her break soon, and hoped we wouldn't end up staying all afternoon.

I had my own hopes as the conversation began, as the executive was intelligent and well-read. He was flattering in his remarks about my music and actually quoted my lyrics. He was sure he was going to sign me.

He had a few questions first, however. I don't remember how he worded the questions, or their order, but they concerned, in a pointed and shocking way, my spiritual well-being, and had little or nothing to do with my music. He said, "These songs seem like they were written by a person who is . . . faithful to his wife!" Then he stared straight into my eyes as if to detect some guilty dilation of my pupils.

I asked him what he meant by that.

He said, "Well, these songs seem like they come from the heart of someone who is . . . intimately involved with his local church, and is probably an elder!"

I started to figure out that he was prompting me or coaxing me into a ritual confession. I disappointed him, I'm afraid, with the way I shrugged off the question. Why was he asking?

"I'd like to just hear you say, 'God has called me into the ministry of music.'"

I told him that that would probably not be my choice of words, and I would feel presumptuous saying something that implies I'm on a first name basis with the Almighty. I told him that I'm not sure what ministry really is, and that whatever it is, God seems to be kind enough to wrap it into our efforts and sometimes wise enough to bestow it in spite of them.

All he wanted was to hear me use the lingo, recite the mantras of evangelical musicians, kids who have been made to feel guilty using their musical abilities, and who, as a result, must justify their talents with post-Jesus movement creeds—formula statements that are as culturally nebulous and stale as the Victorian ones against which that movement originally cried out.

He tried several more times to get me to just say the words. I said that

I would make it a point not to say those particular words, if for no other reason than to get him to think about what they meant.

Being a smart person, he knows I would have to do interviews to sell records for him, and that in those interviews, I would be asked the same types of questions, and I would be expected to toe the party line and echo the same litanies—make the "comforting noise," as McLuhan put it.

I told him I just want to write some more songs and put them on tape. I figure the content of the songs and how I choose to answer for myself is my business. He says he is sorry, even cut to the heart, but he cannot and will not sign me, as, alas, I cannot say the things he wanted to hear.

I say I am sorry he cannot hear the things I'm trying to say.

ON TOUR, JANUARY, 1979

Tonight I played at a coffeehouse/club. It was in an old building, and there were what I must assume were paintings of the Holy Spirit or something on the wall, done quickly in bad tempera. The dressing room was an office of some sort, I think. There was no place to sit. I tuned my guitar and was looking through a possible set list when the man in charge walked in. He said it was time to pray, as the concert was to start in five minutes.

After a ten minute prayer, the gist of which was, "Oh Lord, just sing through Mark tonight and keep him out of the picture altogether," I considered the prospect of lining up a great number of such concerts, then staying at home and sending a cardboard likeness of myself for God to sing through.

I felt like, "why even bother writing songs?" why consult your heart and soul in order to expose it, why subject yourself to the gristmill of life and then try to bleed through a pen when it is all so easily reduced?

Why pray to a god who would rather speak through say, a stone? Too bad that God made so many people who are interested in music and so few stones who are.

Needless to say, when I arrived on stage, I was not in the best of all possible moods. I went through twenty-two songs, opting between each not to say anything. I just sang. Having spent over an hour in this manner, and having for the moment quieted the rage inside myself through the therapy of re-living my life on six steel strings, I exited the stage back to the dressing room/office.

Here I was met by the red-faced man in charge who didn't say much, although I heard him clearly. He proceeded onto the stage where he intimated to those present that the man who had just performed could not possibly be a Christian because of the questioning nature of some of the songs and because of the obvious fact that he had not SAID anything, and after all, what is any musician worth who doesn't talk between his songs.

After this information, he proceeded to make up for all I had not said by a gospel presentation seeming to last half a lifetime. He returned red-faced to the dressing room/office, where I still stood, and uttered words to match the color of his face.

Since I had another thirteen gigs to play on the tour, he had decided to take it upon himself to call each of the promoters for those gigs personally and inform them of my infidel status. I knew it would be useless to argue. I know I can be stubborn, but I kept asking myself, as we walked through the cold to his dented yellow Pinto, "what good is music if you have to talk about it?"

Ten years later, I was playing guitar on tour for another artist, staying in a hospitality house in Washington, DC. A young girl was serving us a lunch of chicken and rice with fruit and herbs, and handed me a note at the end of the meal. It turns out she had been present at the concert at that coffee house/club and had listened to the songs and remembered them, and had forgotten what the red-faced man had said altogether.

SWITZERLAND

We were driven to a house atop a hill overlooking the lake of Neuchatel. The autumn light and the thin wind made for a striking light blue color on the surface of the lake, which was further accented by the yellowing leaves in the gardens on the hillsides and the brown-reds of the tile rooftops. We had to climb a couple hundred yards of steps to reach our chalet. It is small with two beds in a loft. There is a nice piano downstairs, but the ground-level floor is a bit chilly for loitering on the ivories.

After resting from the drive and lack of sleep from the long concert the night before, we went to the concert hall for soundcheck. There seemed to be electrical problems—which would persist throughout that night's performance.

After the soundcheck, we talked with members of the local youth-group for about an hour. The church was an old Romanesque structure, and I kept drinking the hot tea we were served to ward off the chill. The walls were damp with condensation. I discovered that the church was adjacent to an excavated Roman-era burial site. We had an hour or two to look around in the musty interior and cold stucco exterior, and the concert began.

There were lyrics projected in German onto the half-rotunda above the stage, onto frescoes so faded they served nicely as a projection screen. Some of the lyrics were out of order, I was told later, and this added a bit of humor for those fluent enough in English to listen and read simultaneously. We talked to a number of people after the concert, most of whom seemed genuinely interested in discussing lyrics, and in discussion itself. A bit different from America.

Afterwards, there was more hot tea and sandwiches. Andrew dropped us off at the chalet in his Citroen, saying, "Tomorrow, I comes to pick you up, then we go eat somebody." I'm sure my German is much worse.

After a number of concerts and meetings, and after talking to quite a number of people to whom we are foreigners, my mind is divided on the way the situation here is as regards the mixture of music with Christianity. Alfredo sometimes seems a typical Christian concert promoter, seeing the concerts as an outreach. Others are simply enamored by American singers who make records in a way that I find rather distasteful. I'm getting a sinking feeling that they are going to make the same mistakes here we have made in America. They want a "Jesus Movement." They want a "Sixties." They see churches, state-run, as cold and heartless places, and the grass to them is greener on the other side of the Atlantic. They want to be like Americans, and I'm afraid they are looking at the culture that has surrounded American fundamentalist Christianity rather than its tenets, and swallowing it whole.

It is a shame, for the national sense of aesthetic here is remarkably higher than back home. As we were in Lucerne, walking across the old wooden bridge in the center of town, I noticed the oil paintings on the apex of each rafter set in the bridge—quite a lot of them. I asked the promoter if they were repainted or cleaned periodically. He replied that they were painted in the 1400s and were cleaned once in the 1700s. I asked him if there were ever any problem with graffiti, and he asked me what that was. "You know, where somebody defaces public property with spray paint, or carves their initials into it," I said.

"Why would somebody want to do something like that?" was his reply.

They don't realize what they have, and what they will give up to emulate America.

But a few of the people I've talked to don't really like Americans. They see us as a bunch of people with John Wayne masks on. This, oddly, gives me hope that they won't make all our mistakes here. There are as yet no Christian record labels—everyone has to compete in the same marketplace, and I envy the healthiness of that. We lost it long ago back home, when the Great Religious Segregation occurred. But I think the strength of the American market will eventually burgeon in here with all its ugliness and affect the way they see things.

I just wish the beautiful Swiss could remain isolationists a bit longer and maintain their own style.

READING BETWEEN THE QUESTIONS

I had sworn I would never do another interview in a Christian publication. I reneged on my promise today. Now, since I am my own record company, I have to take whatever opportunities present themselves in order to promote my music to people who might buy it, so I can keep on doing it. If I had my choice . . .

The interview went fairly well, as such interviews go. At least I didn't feel attacked. There are two attitudes prevalent in the Christian press as it relates to the music business. Conservatives tend to take one's spiritual temperature, and I must admit that procedure often feels like it is done with a thermometer of the non-oral sort.

The second attitude is one of "We can be as cool as those secular publications," in which the interviewer wants to feel like an outsider in order to be as cool as he considers the interviewee to be. Both attitudes are, it seems to me, useless, but these folks make their livings that way, and their magazines might help me sell a few records.

Life is much more of a compromise than I ever imagined. In printed media, there is always the angle to consider. No matter what you say, words can be put in your mouth, and usually are, by those of the conservative persuasion. The particulars of what you say are not important. It's the smell of the interview that seems to matter to them, and if you read between the questions, the primary question seems to be: "But are you really a Christian?" The interview becomes a litmus test. It strikes me as people greeting like dogs. It is a waste of time if you can't move on from that point.

It is especially difficult if a song you have written is hard for them to understand. The unfamiliar causes them to panic, and they want to see the results of your saliva test before they will allow for the possibility that what you have written might be valid.

Funny, if you go through the litmus test for a while, then they will start to listen to you sometimes. But only so far as the next thing you say that sounds unfamiliar to them. I believe this attitude is fostered by fear, and condemns anyone who dares to be a bit different to be assumed guilty until he can prove himself innocent.

I can't count the number of times I have felt hurt inside—that it couldn't just be accepted that I was a Christian—that I had to prove it on their terms and with their words. They can slant the interview any way they wish in their magazine, and make you look like an infidel or a hero.

Dealing with "cool" interviewers can be just as frustrating. People can be so taken with music that they ascribe to it more importance than it has. They find more than is actually there sometimes. With all the new "Christian alternative" labels springing up everywhere, the attitude seems to be: "Hey, we can be just as cool as those bands in the secular world."

It's sad that the Christian music environment has not given these musicians enough of a feeling of self-worth to the point that they feel they must hide their identity on the fringes and emulate some other pop phenomenon in order to justify their musicianship.

Some try to make the jump to a major label deal. But the music business is no more about truth on the outside of the Christian ghetto than it is on the inside.

Music is a product and a product only in this economic structure. If you find something else in it, then all the better—they'll use that as the angle and sell it to you in larger quantities. But it is nice to see real musical art exist in spite of all these things. The joke is on the business somehow, by God's grace, if you look real hard. It is the people who understand these things, Christian or no, to whom I am grateful after an interview, because usually we are still finding things to talk about after the interview is over.

On a tour a few years ago, I played in a lot of bars. Most people think that bar owners only use music as a come-on in order to sell drinks. But by the end of the tour, I had met a lot of owners of bars and clubs that I really respected—there were so many lovely individual stories.

One couple's lifelong dream had been to open a bar where there could be music they liked and people to hear it. They were not Christians, but they did not mind that I was. They showed us a bit of the town and told us a bit about their lives, and were quite endearing.

Why is it that I felt closer to them than I have with most promoters at Christian colleges I've played? Perhaps we have more in common by virtue of our common humanity than we have differences by virtue of our religions. Maybe the problem in Christian media stems from being taught a reversal of these things, so that a "them and us" mentality takes hold of us, and we have to go on greeting like dogs to make sure that we are on the "us" side of the fence.

CONFESSIONAL

Music is a solace for me now. As I age, contrary to common sense, I am more and more drawn into it and apt to spend more of my waking and some of my sleeping hours thinking about it, or just feeling about it. It is my escape. What with earthquakes, medical insurance, taxes, correspondence, fatherhood, traffic, lack of job security, I am increasingly irresponsible, it seems, in that I take on the mantle of Peter Pan and follow the second star to the right directly between a pair of speakers, or to the case that holds my mandolin. To feel the wood in my hands makes up for a variety of stress and pressures that I probably should spend more time worrying about, things which never go away regardless of how caught-up you feel. They do go away for chunks of time, though, when I am making music of some sort.

I don't know why the attraction is so strong. I am surprised haphazardly by the same deep resonances inside when I find myself thumbing through a magazine and come upon a particularly striking photograph, or see a painting hanging in an out-of-the-way place. I'm drawn into the mood of those photographs or paintings—I think of feelings I have had when stopping my car on a cross country drive in the desert and standing there in the windy loneliness for a while, hearing nothing, seeing shadows, the subtle color differences in different heights and textures of blowing grasses, feeling the extreme largeness of the outdoor room and its horizonless walls; or I think of the feeling of waking up in the musty woods with daylight barely filtering through motionless leaves overhead, the dampness on the ground felt as an unheard thud; or the smell of piñon wood burning, and the cold air carrying it into my nostrils, as the sun drapes red dirt and rocks with the crimson curtain of a melancholy sunset; or the feeling of standing helplessly in a fluorescent hospital corridor, watching the minute hand of a cheap wall clock stand still while my Daddy dies a grueling death and steps into eternity.

The primacy of these feelings impels me to capture them, and preserve them in my memory forever; to conjure the magic of something good waiting around the corner, over the hill, tomorrow, on the morning of the resurrection.

Music is my job, so it does not always fulfill this purpose, but usually, at the least, it sets me on the path to it. It is difficult at best to reveal one's true self to those who are closest, much less to friends and acquaintances and audiences. But when you are able to catch a glimpse of your true self, of the beauty you have felt and the despair you have been burdened with, that is something that transcends the antiseptic responsibility of making the daily ends meet.

I wish sometimes that I just didn't have to think about any of this, and could drone away my life. It would be easier. I have worked in a factory, and one becomes a bit hypnotized after some time to the point where all one can think about is going home, watching TV, having a beer and going to bed—so the cycle may be repeated. The music business can be like this, but I find myself ever thankful that I have not lost the resonances inside when the music is right. I have no idea how we have made ends meet thus far, as I am rather useless in other areas. But increasingly, writing brings about a catharsis of my own terror and pity. It is something I have to do. Dare I say that it becomes an experience of worship for me at times?

When you can see through the fog for an instant, and you understand haltingly and briefly what good is, and how God is connected with that, it cannot help but put a hell of a perspective on things you perceive as problems, and help you discover multiple ways in which you have been numb. For that brief moment you feel that God's in His heaven and all's right with the world.

I've tried to explain this to those family members who are not of the artistic persuasion, and they find it difficult to understand. I find it difficult to understand myself, and sometimes wonder if normal people can feel these strong pluckings of the celestial strings.

Maybe those inclined towards the arts are so spiritually retarded to a degree that we must go through the whole process of cathartic expression just to discover how we really feel. Artistic expression might be seen as a Darwinian protection device for the psyche of fragile individuals, for whom sensuous contact with the outside world is too much to bear, and is repressed, and must be brought up and thrust out into the open from time to time at great effort in order for them to simply survive emotionally.

I only know that I am cursed with doing it.

I must at least tell somebody, even only God and myself, what I have seen and felt. As soon as I think of how I have felt, the words to describe it come, and only need to be written down; the melody is there, and it works its way out of my larynx onto a cheap dictation recorder, to be forgotten or to be listened to later and fleshed out as part of the job.

Maybe I'm just a selfish maniac who is wasting his time trying to transfer feelings which perhaps no one cares about onto a fretboard and a piece of magnetic tape. Maybe it's the modern petroglyph, or the modern way to write on the wall of your cave: "I was here." Maybe it is a cry to God about how much I hate the bad things and how much I love the good things.

{APPENDIX 2}

TIMELINE/COMPLETE DISCOGRAPHY/COVERS

TIMELINE

1951
- Dec. 16: Mark Heard born in Macon, Georgia.

1956
- Mark starts piano lessons.

1969
- Having embraced Christianity in high school, Mark forms his first "christian rock" band (he played in other rock and R&B bands throughout high school).

1970
- Mark graduates from high school in Macon and moves to Athens to attend the University of Georgia, pursuing a degree in film and television production.
- Mark forms the band Infinity Plus Three and becomes extensively involved with Campus Crusade for Christ.*

1971
- Infinity Plus Three records *Setting Yesterday Free.*

1972
- *Setting Yesterday Free* released.
- Mark leaves Infinity Plus Three and starts performing solo.
- Columbia Records offers Mark a recording contract, but since Mark isn't 21 yet, he needs parental approval. Mark's father, John, refuses to sign the contract,

believing that Mark is better off staying in college.*

• Mark meets Pat Terry.*

1973

• Mark meets Chuck Long and records with Ron Moore for the first time (on Ron's Airborne album).

• In the summer of this year, Mark travels to Ithaca, N.Y., for a Campus Crusade event, where he meets Janet Currin.

1974

• Mark graduates from the University of Georgia. He takes his first job, teaching a Bible and theology class at First Presbyterian Day School in Macon.

• Mark produces a documentary about Pat Terry.

1975

• Mark releases his first solo album, *Mark Heard,* on Ron Moore's Airborne label.

• Summer: Mark and Chuck Long travel to Europe to attend Francis Schaeffer's L'Abri study center. Mark would return there several more times.

• Mark takes a job at Spinks Co. in East Point, Georgia, a suburb of Atlanta. (Mark's main job was assembling scales and automatic chicken feeders; the company also made orthopedic mattresses and other medical devices. Spinks foreman Homer Winslow and his wife, Irene, are immortalized in Mark's song "Happy Cornbread Anniversary" on *Appalachian Melody.*)

1976

• Mark meets Larry Norman and Randy Stonehill and is offered a contract with Solid Rock.

1977

• April 2: Mark marries Janet Currin.

• November: Mark and Janet travel for the first time to Los Angeles, where they meet Tom Howard.

1978

• March: Mark and Janet move to Los Angeles.

• *Mark Heard* reissued as *On Turning to Dust.*

1979

• *Appalachian Melody* released.

1980

• Mark meets Dan Russell.

- Mark returns to L'Abri, along with Janet. *Fingerprint* is recorded and released in Switzerland. Mark spent significant portions of this and the next two years in Europe.

1981
- Mark signs with Home Sweet Home. *Stop the Dominoes* is released.

1982
- *Victims of the Age* is released.
- Mark earns his first producer credits, on the self-titled LP by Swiss band Marchstei and on Pat Terry's *Humanity Gangsters*.

1983
- *Eye of the Storm* is released.
- Mark produces Mänsche for Marchstei and Film at Eleven for Pat Terry.

1984
- Mark builds his own studio, Fingerprint Recorders, in a converted ice-cream truck.
- *Ashes and Light* is released.

1985
- *Mosaics* is released.
- Mark leaves Home Sweet Home Records, which releases *The Best of Mark Heard—Acoustic.*

1986
- Home Sweet Home releases *The Greatest Hits of Mark Heard.*
- WHAT? Records is formed and releases its first album, Tonio K.'s *Romeo Unchained.*
- Mark meets Matthew Dickerson.

1987
- WHAT? Records releases Mark's *Tribal Opera* album under the pseudonym iDEoLA.

1988
- February 18: Rebecca Heard is born.
- Mark works as a music teacher* in addition to his engineering and producing chores.

1989
- Mark tours with Sam Phillips, playing guitar.

1990
- Mark, Chuck Long, and Dan Russell form Fingerprint Records. *Dry Bones Dance* is released.

1991
- *Second Hand* is released.
- Autumn: Mark's father dies.

1992
- *Satellite Sky* is released.
- July 4: Mark suffers a heart attack while performing at the Cornerstone Festival in Illinois.
- July 10: Mark suffers a second heart attack and falls into a coma.
- August 16: Mark dies.

* Unconfirmed date; this is an inference or "best guess" within a year or so.

COMPLETE DISCOGRAPHY

Compiled by Martin Stillion and Dan Kennedy, with the able assistance of Roar Sørenson, Kyle Griffin, Miles O'Neal, Eric and Jason Townsend, Wayne Shuman, Mike Rohlinger, Doug Desmarais, Randy Layton, Jean-Daniel von Lerber, Ed Crabtree, Michael Myer, and Christian Hancock. Album descriptions by Martin Stillion, Roar Sørenson, and Josh Jackson.

1972

Infinity Plus Three
Setting Yesterday Free (LP)
Spirit Records V-1111 (1972) / Fingerprint/Silhouette Records (1998)
Mark's first recording, with a folk band he formed after his conversion to Christianity—around the time he finished high school and entered college. (Mark played with rock and R&B bands in high school, and had a rock band for a while in college in addition to Infinity Plus Three.) Mark wrote six songs; contributed guitar, bass, harmonica, and vocals; and co-produced with Doug Milheim. While this release may sound amateurish 30-plus years later, it was similar in quality to most "Jesus music" of the period, and Mark's lyrics reveal an interest in metaphor, a capacity for introspection, and a careful choice of words. In the liner notes to *Appalachian Melody,* Mark recounted that not long after *Setting Yesterday Free* was released, "I was getting tired of the stereotypes surrounding Christian music, so I left the group and began performing solo." It was not the last time he would make such a decision.

Songs:
All My Trials/Life's Ocean/You/Morning Light/Memory/Friends/Presence of the Lord/Second Best Friend/Not Alone/A Place Inside/Love
The 1998 CD reissue on Fingerprint Records includes the following bonus live tracks: Washed to the Sea/Nothing Is Bothering Me/With Broken Wings/Rise from the Ruins

1973

Ron Moore
Airborne (LP)
Airborn Records AR-1003 (1973) / Hartsong HK 5010 (1979)
"Jesus music" pioneer Ron Moore operated an independent label, Airborn Records, in Mark's hometown of Macon, Georgia. On this album, Mark plays guitar on one song, "Good Mornin' Sunshine."

1975

Mark Heard

Mark Heard (LP)

Airborn Records 751005 (1975) / Fingerprint/Silhouette Records (1998)

Mark's first solo album, released on Ron Moore's Airborn label. Reissued in 1978 as *On Turning to Dust*. Mark's early work is often compared to James Taylor, and the similarities are obvious on this recording. The songwriting is uneven, but a few tunes, notably "On Turning to Dust," foreshadow the brilliance that was to come. Production work, including a string quartet on some tracks, is much better than *Setting Yesterday Free*. Original songs are supplemented with several traditional selections.

Songs:

On Turning to Dust/Dinner at Grandma's/Cabin in Gloryland/A Friend/Abba's Lullaby/Solid Rock/To Diane/Greensleeves/There Is a Fountain/Coming Down the Road/Passion Chorale

The 1998 CD reissue includes the following bonus live tracks: I'm Crying Again/ Stuck in the Middle/The Power of Love/True Love

1978

Mark Heard

On Turning to Dust (LP)

AB Records AB 778 (1978)

Reissue of Mark Heard with different cover art and title.

Ron Moore

Death Defying Leap (LP)

Airborn Records AR 7775 (1978)

Mark sang background vocals, and Pat Terry contributed lead guitar and background vocals.

1979

Mark Heard

Appalachian Melody (LP)

Solid Rock Records SRA 2009 (1979)

Produced by Larry Norman and Mark, *Appalachian Melody* continues in the acoustic, James Taylorish vein established on Mark's debut record, but with more confidence. A few tracks feature Jon Linn's electric blues guitar leads, hinting at new musical directions for Mark. With the possible exception of *Fingerprint*, this is the album that best captures Mark's playful, humorous side. Novelty numbers such as "On the Radio" and "Jonah's Song" provide comic relief from the deeper, introspective dimensions of "Here I Am (Once Again)" and "Sidewalk Soliloquy." This is the only one of Mark's records that has never seen a CD reissue, although

in late 2002 Larry Norman announced that he would be preparing one.
Songs:
On the Radio/Castaway/Bless My Soul/Here I Am (Once Again)/With the Setting Sun/Appalachian Melody/Happy Cornbread Anniversary/Two Trusting Jesus/Jonah's Song/Sidewalk Soliloquy/The Last Time/The Saints

Mark Heard
"Here I Am (Once Again)" b/w "Castaway" (7-inch 45 RPM single)
Solid Rock Records SRS 206 (1979)
Both sides are stereo.

Rock & Religion Radio Show #90, 11/25/1979 (LP)
Sangre Productions
Hosted by Mary Neely, who later founded the Exit Records label in Sacramento, *Rock & Religion* examined spiritual themes in both "secular" and "christian" music. This edition features several interview segments with Mark along with songs from *Appalachian Melody.* Show #89, on the same disc, features Terry Talbot.
Tracks:
Intro—Appalachian Melody/Interview/The Last Time/Interview/Happy Cornbread Anniversary/On the Radio/Interview/Castaway/Interview/Here I Am/Interview/With the Setting Sun/Closing

1980
Mark Heard
Fingerprint (LP)
King's/Palmfrond Records PALM 1001 (1980) / Fingerprint/VIA/Diamante VRD6023 (1995)
Mark's European-only release on the Swiss label Palmfrond Records, produced, engineered, and mixed by Mark. Here Mark continues the transition from acoustic music to rock'n'roll, blending his folky sound with a few electric numbers. Both his razor wit and his sensitive artistry are in full evidence here, and the album contains his first indisputable masterpiece, "All the Sleepless Dreamers." Reissued on CD with new cover art in 1995 on Fingerprint Records, distributed by VIA/Diamante.
Songs:
I'm in Chains/Nowadays/One More Time/Epistle/Just the Same/Well Worn Pages/Gimme Mine/All the Sleepless Dreamers/Negative Charge/Brown-Eyed Sue/Es Tut Mir Leid/Remarks to Mr. McLuhan/Threefold Amen

Larry Norman
Roll Away the Stone (and Listen to the Rock) (LP)
Phydeaux WOOF-999-2 (1980)
Mark played rhythm guitar on this live recording.

Steve Scott
Moving Pictures (unreleased)
Solid Rock (1980)

Englishman Steve Scott, a poet, counselor, essayist, and songwriter, was on Larry Norman's Solid Rock roster in late 1970s/early '80s. Work on *Moving Pictures*, which was to be his debut, began in 1978, but the project was among several Solid Rock albums that never were released. In the liner notes to *Stop the Dominoes*, Mark states that he and Larry were Steve's co-producers. Steve went on to release a number of critically acclaimed albums of art rock, poetry, and electronic tape loops—despite seeing two more of his projects, *Emotional Tourist* and *Rice*, shelved by Exit/A&M in the 1980s. "More Than a Dream" from *Moving Pictures* appears as a bonus track on the CD reissue (by Millenium 8 Distribution) of Steve's *Love In the Western World* album. It's clearly identifiable as a Solid Rock product, with lots of Jon Linn guitar fills and hilarious background vocals—unmistakably Mark and Randy Stonehill.

Randall Waller
Midnight Fire (LP)
Tunesmith TS 6006 (1980)

Mark provided additional engineering.

1981

Mark Heard
Stop the Dominoes (LP)
Home Sweet Home Records R2101 (1981) / HSHMH003 (1999)

Mark's first release on Chris Christian's Home Sweet Home label. (The Home Sweet Home years were some of Mark's most productive in terms of output, but he felt increasingly stifled by the pressure to make what he perceived as artistic compromises.) Rapidly maturing as a songwriter, Mark here develops two of the themes that dominated both his work and his life: a feeling of alienation from both the dominant American culture and the christian subculture ("I'm Crying Again," "Stuck in the Middle") and a hope and longing for truth and God's presence ("To See Your Face"). Produced and arranged by Mark. Reissued on CD in 1999.

Songs:
One of the Dominoes/Stranded at the Station/You Could Lie to Me/One Night Stand/I'm Crying Again/ Stuck in the Middle/Call Me the Fool/I'm in Chains/ Lonely One/To See Your Face

Mark Heard
"One of the Dominoes" (7-inch 45 RPM single)
Home Sweet Home Records 5394

This 45 contains stereo & mono versions of the song. It was packaged in a picture sleeve with lyrics on the front.

1982
Mark Heard
Victims of the Age (LP)
Home Sweet Home Records R2107 (1982) / HSHMH004 (1999)
This album realized all of Mark's lyrical potential, pounding Francis Schaeffer's pulpit of artistic and poetic honesty in the face of the decline of Western culture ("Victims of the Age," "City Life Won't Let Up") and taking christendom to task for its detachment from the world's problems ("Growing Up Blind," "Dancing at the Policeman's Ball," "Some Folks' World," "Nothing Is Bothering Me"). Modern, relevant, sensitive songwriting. Produced and arranged by Mark. Reissued on CD in 1999.

Marchstei
Marchstei (LP)
Philips/Polygram 6367 028 (Switzerland, 1982)
Produced by Mark. Mark's pet nickname for Marchstei was "the Screaming Cheese Band." Jean-Daniel von Lerber of Marchstei was Mark's European concert promoter, and still operates Profile Productions in Switzerland.

Pat Terry
Humanity Gangsters (LP)
Myrrh MSB-6698 (1982)
Produced and arranged by Mark and Pat Terry. Engineered by Mark and Bill Cobb and mixed by Mark. Mark played electric guitar and bass guitar and contributed background vocals, handclaps, and dancing. Photographs and layout by Mark.

1983
Mark Heard
Eye of the Storm (LP)
Home Sweet Home Records/Myrrh MSB 6741 (1983) / HSHMH008 (1999)
Stylistically, this acoustic-oriented release had more in common with Mark's first two albums than with the next three. It even reprised several older songs. *Eye of the Storm* was the most commercially successful of Mark's Home Sweet Home projects, but in many ways it was the last of his albums to make overt concessions to the demands of the CCM marketplace. Standout tracks include "These Plastic Halos," "The Pain That Plagues Creation," and "He Will Listen to You." Produced and arranged by Mark. Reissued on CD in 1999.
Songs:
Eye of the Storm/The Pain That Plagues Creation/Castaway/Well-Worn Pages/

He Will Listen to You/In the Gaze of the Spotlight's Eye/Gimme Mine/These Plastic Halos/No One But You/Moonflower

Mark Heard
"The Pain That Plagues Creation" (7-inch 45 RPM single)
Myrrh M-290 (1983)
Both sides are stereo.

Tom Howard
Unreleased album, co-produced by Mark and Terry Taylor.
Mark and Tom were labelmates at Solid Rock Records and worked frequently together throughout Mark's career.

Marchstei
Mänsche (LP)
Philips/Polygram 6367 043 (Switzerland, 1983)
Produced and engineered by Mark.

Pat Terry
Film at Eleven (LP)
Myrrh MSB 6748 (1983)
Produced and arranged by Mark and Pat Terry, and engineered and mixed by Mark. Mark played guitar, performed background vocals and handclaps, co-wrote the song "The World Around Us," and made "assorted techno-musical contributions" on this overlooked garage-rock classic. When Campus Life ran a review dismissing Pat as a Mark Heard clone, Mark replied with a scathing letter in defense of the album.

1984
Mark Heard
Ashes and Light (LP)
Home Sweet Home Records SPCN 7-01-679706-6 (1984) / HSHMH006 (1999)
Eager to return to rock'n'roll after *Eye of the Storm*, Mark wrote and recorded the *Mosaics* album. But his label asked him for another acoustic record first, in hopes of capitalizing on the (relative) success of *Eye of the Storm*. In five weeks, Mark wrote, recorded, and mixed *Ashes and Light*, working in his new mobile studio, Fingerprint Recorders. The album may have been acoustic, but it wasn't commercial. The ashes—some of Mark's most incisive, acerbic writing to date ("Threw It Away," "We Believe So Well," "Straw Men")—were mitigated by the occasional hopeful ray of light ("I Know What It's Like to Be Loved," "In Spite of Himself," "Washed to the Sea"). Produced and arranged by Mark. Reissued on CD in 1999.
Songs:

The Winds of Time/True Confessions/I Know What It's Like to Be Loved/Washed to the Sea/We Believe So Well/Straw Men/Age of the Broken Heart/Can't See Light/Threw It Away/In Spite of Himself

Mark Heard
"We Believe So Well" b/w same (7-inch 45 RPM single)
Myrrh 9016170154-DJ (1984)
One side is stereo; the other side is mono

Various Artists
The Strait Tapes, Vol. II (cassette)
No label or number. Distributed in the UK.
This cassette-only sampler was part of a series released by *Strait* magazine, a publication of the UK's Greenbelt Festival. It includes Mark's song "Victims of the Age."

Randy Stonehill
Celebrate This Heartbeat (LP)
Myrrh SPCN 7-01-676506-7 (1984)
Engineered by Mark. Recorded and mixed at Fingerprint Recorders. Mark also played electric twelve-string guitar, slide guitar, bass, and harmonica.

Pat Terry
The Silence (LP)
Myrrh SPCN 7-01-679106-8 (1984)
Produced by Mark and Pat Terry, and engineered and mixed by Mark. Mark played bass and contributed background vocals.

1985
Mark Heard
Mosaics (LP)
Home Sweet Home/Myrrh SPCN 7-01-680006-7 (1985) / HSHMH007 (1999)
Recorded in 1983–84, but delayed until after *Ashes and Light*. A decidedly rock album (more so than any up to this point) with a great cover of T-Bone Burnett's "The Power of Love." This was Mark's most focused work of social criticism, and his last studio record for Home Sweet Home. Produced by Mark. Reissued on CD in 1999.
Songs:
With Broken Wings/Schizophrenia/All Is Not Lost/Heart on the Line/He Plays the Game/The Golden Age/The Power of Love/I Want You/It Will Not Be Like This Forever/Miracle

Mark Heard

The Best of Mark Heard—Acoustic (LP)
Home Sweet Home SPCN 7-01-000840-X (1985) / HSHMH005 (1999)
A compilation of acoustic-oriented songs from Mark's Home Sweet Home re-
leases (1981–84), including a new song, "Family Name," written by Bill Batstone.
Reissued on CD in 1999.

Songs:
Family Name/Eye of the Storm/Castaway/In the Gaze of the Spotlight's Eye/Call
Me the Fool/To See Your Face/I'm Crying Again/Some Folks' World/Can't See
Light/True Confessions/Well-Worn Pages/In Spite of Himself

Altar Boys
When You're a Rebel (LP)
Broken SPCN 7-100-30282-X (1985)
Mixed by Mark (credited as Leroy Cahuenga).

David Edwards
Dreams, Tales & Lullabies (LP)
Light/Lexicon LS-5867 (1985) / Light SPCN 5141651212 (1995)
Recorded and mixed by Mark in September 1984. The liner notes of the 1995
CD reissue read: "This release of Dreams, Tales and Lullabies is dedicated to the
memory of Mark Heard, poet to the poets."

Tom Howard and Bill Batstone
One by One (LP)
A&S Records SPCN 7-100-92182-1 (1985)
Engineered and mixed at Fingerprint Recorders by Mark.

Randy Stonehill
Love Beyond Reason (LP)
Myrrh SPCN 7-01-681106-9 (1985)
Engineered and mixed at Fingerprint Recorders by Mark. Mark also played guitar
on "Cross That Line."

Randy Stonehill
Love Beyond Reason Video Album (videocassette)
Myrrh 8015011698 (1985)
Directed by Bob Lauro and audio-engineered and mixed by Mark.

Randy Stonehill
Stonehill (12-inch, 45 RPM EP)
Street Tunes XSTLP 1 (1985) (UK)
Two of this EP's five tracks were recorded at Fingerprint Recorders, and engi-
neered and mixed by Mark. Additional overdubs and remix of a third track were

done at Fingerprint with Mark as remix engineer.

1986

Mark Heard
The Greatest Hits of Mark Heard (LP)
Home Sweet Home 7-01-001039-0 (1986) / HSHMH002 (1999)
A compilation of rock-oriented songs from Mark's Home Sweet Home releases (1981–85) with a wryly oxymoronic title. There are two CD reissues. The first (Home Sweet Home, 1999) retains the original cover art, title, and track order; the second (BCI, 1999) shortens the title to Greatest Hits, changes the cover art and track order, and adds "Eye of the Storm" and "Everybody Loves a Holy War."
Songs:
Heart of Hearts/The Winds of Time/Stranded at the Station/Threw It Away/ Victims of the Age/Stuck in the Middle/The Golden Age/One of the Dominoes/ Dancing at the Policeman's Ball/One Night Stand/Nothing Is Bothering Me/ Faces in Cabs

Tonio K.
Romeo Unchained (LP, CD)
What? Records/A&M WR 8340 (1986). CD: What? 7-01-684261-4.
Engineered by Mark (as one of several).

1987

iDEoLA
Tribal Opera (LP, CD)
What? Records/A&M 7-01-684906-6 (1987). CD: What? 7-01-684961-9.
Mark took the pseudonym "iDEoLA" for this electronic tour de force on the new What? label. Heavy on the digital samples, synths, and drum machines, this album sounded nothing like any of his work before or since. Mark had already established a reputation as a formidable songwriter, but on *Tribal Opera* his skills took a quantum leap forward. It's a must have, with "How to Grow Up Big and Strong," "Hold Back Your Tears," and "Go Ask the Dead Man" leading the pack. Recorded and produced by Mark at Fingerprint LA. (Mark apparently renamed his studio after moving it from a mobile unit to a shed behind his house.)
Songs:
I Am an Emotional Man/Is It Any Wonder/Watching the Ship Go Down/Talk to Me/Go Ask the Dead Man/Love Is Bigger Than Life/How to Grow Up Big and Strong/Everybody Dances/Why Can't We Just Say No/Hold Back Your Tears

iDEoLA
"Is It Any Wonder?"
What? Records/A&M (1987) SP-17448 (12-inch 33 1/3 RPM single) / 2914 (7-inch

45 RPM single, both sides stereo) / CD-17447 (CD single)
Also released as a video for MTV.

Various Artists
CD Tuneup No. 3 (CD)
The Album Network (1987)
Radio Sampler CD from June 22, 1987. Contains the iDEoLA track "Watching the Ship Go Down." Other artists on this sampler include Los Lobos, The Fixx, Pat Metheny, INXS, and comic Jackie Mason.

Various Artists
Home Sweet Home's Greatest Hits (CD)
  Home Sweet Home 7010026718 (1987)
  Contains Mark's "Eye of the Storm."

1988
  The Choir
  Chase the Kangaroo (CD)
  Myrrh 7-01-686961-X (1988)
  Recorded by Mark (as one of several).

  Phil Keaggy
  Phil Keaggy and Sunday's Child (CD)
  Myrrh 7016876616 (1988)
  Mark was one of several engineers on this project, and some of the tracks were recorded at Fingerprint LA. Mark contributed on five songs (background vocals on four songs, and guitar and keyboards on one song each), and wrote "Everything Is Alright" and "I Always Do."

  Olivia Newton-John
  The Rumour (CD)
  MCA 76732-6245-2 (1988)
  Mark wrote the song "Big and Strong," as well as contributing guitar, keyboards, and programming.

  Larry Norman
  The Best of the Second Trilogy (limited edition cassette)
  Phydeaux ARF-023 (1988)
  Mark mixed the "downtown dub" version of "Soul on Fire," which also appears on the 1997 CD version of Larry's *White Blossoms from Black Roots*.

  Steve Taylor
  The Best We Could Find (+3 That Never Escaped) (CD)

Sparrow SPD 1180 (1988)
Mark mixed "Down Under."

1989
The Choir
Wide-Eyed Wonder (CD)
Myrrh 7016885615 (1989)
Mixed by Mark (as one of several); Mark also contributed background vocals on three songs, played bass guitar and autoharp on one song, and produced two songs. In addition, he directed the promo video for the song "Robin Had a Dream."

Phil and John
Don't Look Now (It's the Hallelujah Brothers) (CD)
Word WHAD 1259 (1989)
Mark engineered, as well as playing electric guitar on five songs and acoustic guitar on one song.

Randy Stonehill
Return to Paradise (CD)
Myrrh 701 6881 61 X (1989)
Produced by Mark with Randy Stonehill. Recorded and mixed at Fingerprint LA by Mark, who also played mandolin, accordion, electric guitar, bass, and tambourine, and wrote "Strong Hand of Love."

Various Artists
Adventures in the Land of Big Beats and Happy Feets (CD)
Myrrh 7016893618 (1989)
Remixes of songs by Philip Bailey, Amy Grant ("Wise Up"), the Imperials, Steve Taylor ("Svengali"), Kim Boyce, Russ Taff, Sheila Walsh, and Randy Stonehill ("Cold Rock the Groove"), as well as an unreleased song, "Jericho," by iDEoLA (a.k.a. Mark Heard). Remixes, edits, and link music by Mark (credited as Lee Cahuenga).

Various Artists
Twelve New Faces (CD)
Myrrh 7016883612 (1989)
A sampler CD featuring one song each from twelve emerging artists. Three of them (Brooks Williams, Pierce Pettis, and Phil Madeira) went on to bigger and better things; the rest you've probably never heard of. Mark mixed songs for three of the artists: Reigh Giglio (now recording under the name "Raphael" and co-pastoring a church in Nashville with Michael W. Smith), Wil Comstock, and Open City. Mark also mixed and produced three others: Brooks Williams, Two

Tru, and Milo Carter. Brooks has had a prolific career as a singer/songwriter, but never worked with Mark as producer apart from "Mystery" on *Twelve New Faces*. (A different version of the song appears on Brooks' *Dead Sea Café* CD.) Mark had produced several demo tracks for Two Tru, a Boston-based duo featuring the talents of Lauren Passarelli and Cindy Brown, who formed their own label, Feather Record, in 1989 and released an album, *Among the Ruins*. However, their song "Tell Me Your Idea," produced by Mark, appears only on *Twelve New Faces*. Milo Carter, a singer-songwriter, guitarist, and prime mover behind the L.A.-based band The Lucky Stiffs, had tracked material at Fingerprint several times during the 1980s with Mark producing (Mark mentions Milo in the liner notes of Ashes and Light), but his song "Line My Streets with Gold" on Twelve New Faces was the only one of those tracks to receive a major-label release.

1990
Mark Heard
Dry Bones Dance (CD)
Fingerprint Records 9001 FCD (1990) / Fingerprint/Via/Diamante VRD6020 (1995)

The first of Mark Heard's final trilogy of albums on his own label, Fingerprint Records. Unencumbered at last by commercial pressures, his songwriting took another astonishing leap, becoming increasingly honest, seeking, poignant, and raw on these three final works. *On Dry Bones Dance,* he revels in an earthy Americana with country rock and Cajun influences, complementing the wry candor of the lyrics. Powerful, emotional, truthful. "Strong Hand of Love," "Lonely Road," "Rise from the Ruins," and "House of Broken Dreams" could hold their own against an equal number of songs from any other "alt-country" writer—or any writer. Produced by Mark, co-produced by Dan Russell.

Songs:
Rise from the Ruins/The Dry Bones Dance/House of Broken Dreams/Our Restless Hearts/Nobody's Looking/All She Wanted Was Love/Strong Hand of Love/ How Many Tears/Lonely Road/Waiting for a Reason/Everything Is Alright/Awake in the Nighttime/Mercy of the Flame/Fire

The Choir
Circle Slide (CD)
Myrrh 7016903613 (1990)
Mark sang background vocals on "About Love."

Randy Stonehill
Until We Have Wings (CD)
Myrrh 7016906612 (1990)
Produced, recorded, and mixed at Fingerprint LA by Mark, who also played

acoustic and electric guitars, bass, and keyboards, and co-wrote "Faithful"—credited to Giovanni Audiori.

1991
Mark Heard
Second Hand (CD)
Fingerprint Records 9102 FCD (1991) / Fingerprint VRD6021 (1995)

Plaintive, passionate, heartbreaking, and hopeful music is colored by warm, acoustic production—all of which dims in comparison to the lyrics, some of the best pure songwriting ever put on tape. Mark shifted his lyrical focus to his own immediate family and came up with a set of intensely beautiful and personal songs—clearly inspired by his wife Janet ("Love Is Not the Only Thing") and daughter Rebecca ("Another Good Lie"), but universally true of just about every relationship in late 20th-century America. Includes provocative ballads such as "Nod Over Coffee," "Lonely Moon," and "Look Over Your Shoulder." Produced by Mark, co-produced by Dan Russell.

Songs:

Nod Over Coffee/Lonely Moon/Worry Too Much/Look Over Your Shoulder/She Don't Have a Clue/Talking in Circles/Love Is Not the Only Thing/I Just Wanna Get Warm/Another Good Lie/All Too Soon/It's Not Your Fault/I'm Looking Through You/What Kind of Friend/The Ways of Men

Mark Heard
Fingerprints in Dust: A Sampler (cassette)
Fingerprint Records FKS-S-91 (1991)

Demo cassette compiled for the purpose of shopping Mark's music to major labels. Produced by Mark. Not released commercially.

Songs:

Nod Over Coffee/Satellite Sky (Rough Mix)/Dry Bones Dance/House of Broken Dreams/Tip of My Tongue (Rough Mix)/Lonely Moon/Love Is So Blind (Rough Mix)/I Just Wanna Get Warm

Billy Batstone
A Little Broken Bread (CD)
Maranatha! CD08776 (1991)

Mark produced and played harmonica.

Garth Hewitt
Lonesome Troubadour (CD)
Myrrh/UK MYRCD 1279 (1991) (UK)

Produced, recorded, and mixed by Mark at Fingerprint LA. Mark played electric guitars, dulcimer guitar, accordion, mandolin, Hammond, and autoharp, and contributed background vocals.

Julie Miller
He Walks Through Walls (CD)
Myrrh 7016928616 (1991)
 Mark sang background vocals (with Victoria Williams) on "Just Want You."

Pierce Pettis
Tinseltown (CD)
High Street 72902 10311-2 (1991)
 Produced, recorded, and mixed at Fingerprint LA by Mark, who also played electric guitars, mandolin, keyboards, and autoharp, and contributed background vocals.

Tom Prasada-Rao
Incoming (CD)
Crossroads CRD1115901 (1991)
 Recorded, produced, engineered, and mixed by Mark, who also sang background vocals and played various instruments, including mandolin, accordion, electric guitar, organ, bass, kalimba, whistle, bass drum, and tambourine.

1992
Mark Heard
Satellite Sky (CD)
Fingerprint/Enclave FLD 9751 (1992) / Fingerprint VRD6022 (1995) / Paste PM11 (2003)
 Mark's last studio recording. 15 songs, electrified and heartfelt. Handling his guitar, accordion, and 1939 National Reso-Phonic "Silvo" electric mandolin as though they were his last hope for redemption, Mark developed a sound that matched his frenetic lyrics. Highlights include the poignant "Orphans of God," "Satellite Sky," "Tip of My Tongue," and Mark's ode to his recently deceased father, "Treasure of the Broken Land." Produced by Mark, and co-produced by Dan Russell and Jim Scott.
Songs:
 Tip of My Tongue/Satellite Sky/Big Wheels Roll/Orphans of God/Another Day in Limbo/Language of Love/Freight Train to Nowhere/Long Way Down/A Broken Man/Love Is So Blind/Hammers and Nails/We Know Too Much/Lost on Purpose/Nothing But the Wind/Treasure of the Broken Land
 The 2003 Paste reissue contains one additional song: She's Not Afraid

Various Artists
The Compassion Project (multimedia box set)
(no label or number) (1992)

Contains a video, two books, and a cassette that includes Mark's "Some Folks' World."

Various Artists
Legacy II: A Collection of Singer Songwriters (CD)
High Street/Windham Hill Records 72902/10314-2 (1992)
  A collection of 13 songs from different singer/songwriters, including Mark's song "Look Over Your Shoulder," taken from the album *Second Hand.*

Various Artists
At the Foot of the Cross, Vol. 1: Clouds, Rain, Fire (CD)
Glasshouse Records 7014771027 (1992)
  Mark mixed, sang, and played guitar on "My Redeemer Lives" on this masterpiece assembled by Derri Daugherty and Steve Hindalong of The Choir. (On *At the Foot of the Cross, Vol. 2* [Myrrh, 1995], the fade of the song "The Winds" pays a tribute to Mark, as a portion of his "My Redeemer Lives" is reprised.)

John Austin
The Embarrassing Young (CD)
Glasshouse 7014701029 (1992)
  Recorded, engineered, mixed, and produced by Mark at Fingerprint LA. Mark played accordion, mandolin, and Gretsch guitar and did the drum programming (as well as whistle and various noises).

John Fischer
Wide Angle (CD)
Enclave Entertainment FL9750 (1992)
  Produced and engineered by Mark. In 1999 Silent Planet Records reissued this album as *Some Folks' World* with three additional songs produced by David Miner, including Fischer's cover of Mark's "Some Folks' World."

Harrod and Funck
Dreams of the Color Blind (CD)
Heated Brick Records HF75425 (1992)
  Produced, engineered, recorded and mixed at Fingerprint by Mark during May/June 1992. Mark played electric guitar, acoustic and electric mandolin, accordion, keyboards, percussion, kalimba, and "swamp gas." The liner notes read, "This record is dedicated to the loving memory of Mark Heard."

Jacob's Trouble
... Let the Truth Run Wild (CD)
Alarma FL9257 (1992)
  Produced and engineered by Mark, who also did background vocals on one song

and played mandolin on another.

Reverend Dan Smith
Just Keep Goin' On (CD)
Glasshouse Records 7014702025 (1992) / Word/Epic EK 52989
Mark contributed background vocals, along with Victoria Williams, on "When Your Time Comes to Die."

Vigilantes of Love
Killing Floor (CD)
Fingerprint 7-5020-2 (1992)
Produced by Mark, Peter Buck of REM, and V.O.L. Engineered by Mark and John Keane, and mixed by Mark at Fingerprint.

1993

Mark Heard
High Noon (CD)
Fingerprint/Epic/Myrrh 7016978613 (1993)
A compilation from Mark's three Fingerprint releases, including three previously unreleased songs ("She's Not Afraid," "No," and "Shaky Situation"), as well as an alternate version of "What Kind of Friend."
The recordings feature the talents of brilliant musicians such as Buddy and Julie Miller, Sam Phillips, Byron Berline (former national fiddle champion and member of Bill Monroe's Blue Grass Boys), Burleigh Drummond of Ambrosia, Chapman Stick player Fergus Jemison Marsh (a longtime associate of Bruce Cockburn) and Michael Been of The Call, as well as many other great musicians. Co-produced by Dan Russell and Buddy Miller.
Songs:
Strong Hand of Love/I Just Wanna Get Warm/Look Over Your Shoulder/My Redeemer Lives/Another Day in Limbo/She's Not Afraid/The Dry Bones Dance/ House of Broken Dreams/Everything Is Alright/Hammers and Nails/Love Is So Blind/Nod Over Coffee/Love Is Not the Only Thing/No/Shaky Situation/Orphans of God/What Kind of Friend/Treasure of the Broken Land

Mark Heard
High Noon (CD single)
Myrrh 9012776155 (1993)
Promotional CD single featuring three tracks: "My Redeemer Lives," "She's Not Afraid" (duet with Julie Miller), and "Treasure of the Broken Land."

Mark Heard
Reflections of a Former Life (CD)
Home Sweet Home 7-90113-275-2 (1993) / HSHMH001 (1999)

A compilation of songs from Mark's Home Sweet Home releases (1981–85), as well as a couple of songs from Fingerprint. No new material; the song "All the Sleepless Dreamers" is mistakenly listed as "Carry On." Executive producer: Chris Christian.

Songs:
Stranded at the Station/Dancing at the Policeman's Ball/Threw It Away/Heart of Hearts/The Winds of Time/Stuck in the Middle/Eye of the Storm/Family Name/One of the Dominoes/Nothing Is Bothering Me/Carry On/Brown-Eyed Sue

Various Artists
WAL Paper Sampler (cassette)
Word 9016987290 (1993)
Cassette-only compilation featuring Mark's song "Treasure of the Broken Land."

The Choir
Kissers and Killers (CD)
Never Say Never Songs TCCD 2000 (1993)
Mark played accordion on the song "Let the Sky Fall" (recorded in 1990). The song was dropped when this demo CD was reissued under the title *Speckled Bird*. Liner notes read, "Forever live the beautiful spirit of our dear friend, Mark."

Randy Stonehill
Stories (CD)
Myrrh 7016970612 (1993)
Several songs in this collection were produced by Mark. Liner notes read, "This record is dedicated with love to the memory of John Mark Heard, who always told the true story."

Vigilantes of Love
Jugular (CD)
Fingerprint 9205 FCD (1993)
This reissue on Fingerprint Records contains all the original songs from V.O.L.'s 1990 debut, digitally remastered, plus two new bonus tracks from the *Killing Floor* sessions. Additional engineering, mixing, and mastering by Mark Heard. Bonus tracks produced by Mark, Peter Buck, and V.O.L. Engineered by Mark and mixed at Fingerprint.

1994
Pam Dwinell Miner
Pam Dwinell Miner (cassette)
Cadillac Fund Productions (no number) (1994)
Mark engineered and/or mixed several tracks, contributed harmony vocals on "I Could Tell a Story" and "Under the Sun," and played mandolin on "If It's True."

Pam also sings Mark's "Look Over Your Shoulder" with Randy Stonehill on this promotional cassette. Many of the tracks found their way onto *(These Could've Been My) Greatest Hits,* her 2001 release (as Kate Miner).

Various Artists
Strong Hand of Love: A Tribute to Mark Heard (CD)
Fingerprint/Epic/Myrrh 701697961X (1994)

Seventeen artists covering Mark's songs. Billboard stated: "Taken as a whole, the collection remind us once again what a brilliant poet Heard was, and what a devastating loss his passing has been to music in general. Unqualified recommendation." The CD was nominated for Best Rock Gospel Album in the 37th annual Grammy Awards in 1994. Produced by Dan Russel. Grammy nominated compilation. Prior to the release of the CD, there was a promotional cassette version of *Strong Hand of Love* with two extra tracks (Harrod & Funck's "Worry Too Much" and Glenn Kaiser & Darrell Mansfield's "Threw It Away") both of which later appeared on the *Orphans of God* collection.

Songs:

Kevin Smith—Lonely Moon/Michael Been—We Know Too Much/Dan Russell—I Just Wanna Get Warm/Bruce Cockburn—Strong Hand of Love/Kate Taylor—Satellite Sky/Phil Keaggy—I Always Do/Pierce Pettis—Nod Over Coffee/Victoria Williams—What Kind of Friend/Bruce Carroll—Castaway/Rich Mullins—Big and Strong/Ashley Cleveland—It's Not Your Fault/Tonio K.—Another Day in Limbo/Randy Stonehill & Kate Miner—Look Over Your Shoulder/Vigilantes of Love—Freight Train to Nowhere/The Choir—Tip of My Tongue/Buddy & Julie Miller—Orphans of God/Chagall Guevara—Treasure of the Broken Land

Various Artists
Strong Hand of Love (videocassette)
Fingerprint Records/Word 8015206693 (1994)

Approximately 50 minutes long, this video contains footage from Mark's last concert on July 4, 1992, and his music videos for "Is It Any Wonder" and "Treasure of the Broken Land." It also features musical performances—such as outtakes from Mark's Fingerprint sessions—and interviews with several artists and friends, including Bruce Cockburn, Michael Been, Victoria Williams, Dan Russell, Bill Mallonee of Vigilantes of Love, Bruce Carroll, Phil Keaggy, Bob Bennett, Buddy and Julie Miller, Pierce Pettis, Steve Taylor, Randy Stonehill, and Pat Terry. Excerpts from the Mark Heard Memorial Benefit Concert at Belmont University in Nashville (January 1993) are included as well.

Various Artists
Strong Hand of Love: The Radio Special (CD)
Fingerprint 9106 (1994)

The Strong Hand of Love Radio Special as aired on WXPN's "World Café" in 1994. This 70-minute tribute to Mark Heard includes music by Mark as well as interviews with artists such as Bruce Cockburn, Sam Phillips, Michael Been of The Call, and Bill Mallonee of Vigilantes of Love, among others. Bruce Cockburn's acoustic version of "Closer to the Light," written in memory of Mark, is available only on this promotional CD.

1995

Various Artists
Essential 80's Christian Collection: Rock Gospel Classics (CD)
K-Tel International 34802 (1995)
This compilation CD is a bit unusual in that it contains both a Mark Heard track ("Victims of the Age") and an iDEoLA track ("Is It Any Wonder").

Various Artists
Via & Swirle Sampler Disc (CD)
Via Records DPROVR95002 (1995)
A sampler from the short-lived Via label, which had a distribution arrangement with Fingerprint Records in the mid-1990s. Mark's song "Tip of My Tongue" is included.

The Choir
Love Songs and Prayers (a Retrospective) (CD)
Myrrh 7017000617 (1995)
Mark produced "A Million Years" and "All Night Long."

1996

Various Artists
Orphans of God (double CD)
Fingerprint 9601 FCD (1996)
A double CD featuring 34 artists performing Mark's songs, including Victoria Williams, Buddy and Julie Miller, Bruce Cockburn, the Williams Brothers, Vigilantes of Love, Daniel Amos, and Phil Keaggy. Fourteen tracks from the *Strong Hand of Love* album appear on this album as well.

Songs (Disc 1):
Buddy & Julie Miller—Orphans of God/Michael Been—We Know Too Much/ Vigilantes of Love—Freight Train to Nowhere/Ashley Cleveland—It's Not Your Fault/Dan Russell—I Just Wanna Get Warm/Kate Taylor—Satellite Sky/Pat Terry—Mercy of the Flame/Brooks Williams—Rise from the Ruins/Bruce Cockburn—Strong Hand of Love/Victoria Williams—What Kind of Friend/The Williams Brothers—House of Broken Dreams/Tom Prasado-Rao—Tip of My Tongue/Phil Keaggy—Everything Is Alright/Olivia Newton John—Big and

Strong/Big Faith—All She Wanted Was Love/hezze—Another Good Lie/Chagall Guevara—Treasure of the Broken Land

Songs (Disc 2):

Kevin Smith—Lonely Moon/Harrod and Funck—Worry Too Much/bob—Fire/ John Austin—Big Wheels Roll/Parmin Sisters—Rise from the Ruins/Iain—Watching the Ship Go Down/Tonio K—Another Day in Limbo/Carolyn Arends—Love Is So Blind/Pierce Pettis—Nod Over Coffee/Ramona Silver—Remarks to Mr. McLuhan/Swinging Steaks—Long Way Down/Randy Stonehill & Kate Miner—Look Over Your Shoulder/Glenn Kaiser & Darrell Mansfield—Threw It Away/ Colin Linden—The Dry Bones Dance/The Choir—Tip of My Tongue/DA—Strong Hand of Love/Marvin Etzioni—Hammers and Nails

Randy Stonehill
Our ReCollections (CD)
Word 7013525367 (1996)

Mark produced several songs in this collection.

Vigilantes of Love
V.O.L. (CD)
Warner Resound 9 46309-2 (1996)

Mark produced several songs in this collection.

1997
Various Artists
Demonstrations of Love (CD)
Prism/ESA Records (no number)

Mark's "Tip of My Tongue" appears on this benefit compilation released by *Prism* magazine, the publication of Evangelicals for Social Action. The song differs from the version released on *Satellite Sky*, in that it has an introduction taken from Mark's home demo. The disc also contains Ramona Silver's cover of Mark's "Remarks to Mr. McLuhan," as well as Randy Stonehill's "Mark's Song," written in memory of Mark and available only here.

Tonio K.
Olé (CD)
Gadfly 233 (1997)

Additional engineering by Mark (as one of several). *Olé* was recorded in 1989 as a follow-up to Tonio K.'s *Notes from the Lost Civilization,* but was shelved when What? Records folded and its parent company, A&M, was sold. Eight years later it was finally released on Gadfly, a Vermont-based folk label.

Larry Norman
White Blossoms from Black Roots (CD)

Solid Rock SRD-041 (1997)

Reissue of SRD-030 with new tracks, one of which is Mark's "ghetto dub remix" of "Soul on Fire."

1999

Mark Heard

Greatest Hits (CD)

BCI Music BCCD1103 (1999)

Reissue of *The Greatest Hits of Mark Heard* with different track order and artwork, and two additional tracks.

Songs:

Heart of Hearts/Winds of Time/Stranded at the Station/Threw It Away/Dancing at the Policeman's Ball/One Night Stand/Eye of the Storm/One of the Dominoes/Victims of the Age/Nothing Is Bothering Me/Faces in Cabs/Golden Age/Stuck in the Middle/Everybody Loves a Holy War

Various Artists

Dakota (film soundtrack) (CD)

Home Sweet Home (1999)

Chris Christian's publishing company, the Las Colinas Group, produced the music for this 1988 film featuring Lou Diamond Phillips, and Chris reports that a soundtrack CD was released on Home Sweet Home Records in 1999. Mark's "Dancing at the Policeman's Ball" was used in the film and appears on the track list for the CD as well. Available only at the Home Sweet Home Web site.

John Fischer

Some Folks' World (CD)

Silent Planet Records SPR0601 (1999)

A reissue of *Wide Angle* (Enclave Entertainment, 1992) with three additional songs, including Fischer's cover of Mark's "Some Folks' World." The tracks from *Wide Angle* were produced and engineered by Mark.

2000

Mark Heard

Mystery Mind (CD)

Fingerprint Records FP 0001 (2000)

This benefit CD includes two live tracks from Mark's final concert at Cornerstone in 1992 ("Freight Train to Nowhere" and "Orphans of God") and six songs recorded live in concert at Calvary Chapel in 1982, as well as four demos: the previously unreleased songs "Mystery Mind" (an instant Heard classic—truly a sparkling gem) and "Let Freedom Ring" as well as "Mercy of the Flame" and "I Just Wanna Get Warm." The CD also includes clips from a fascinating interview with Mark. *Mystery Mind* was released on CD-R to benefit the Heard Family Fund. All proceeds from its sale support Mark's family as well as perpetuating the legacy of his work.

Songs:

Mystery Mind (demo)/Interview One/Mercy of the Flame (demo)/Interview/I Just Wanna Get Warm (demo)/Interview Three/Let Freedom Ring (demo)/Freight Train to Nowhere (live)/Orphans of God (live)/Interview Four/Nothing Is Bothering Me (live)/Some Folks' World (live)/Growing Up Blind (live)/Dancing at the Policeman's Ball (live)/Everybody Loves a Holy War (live)/Heart of Hearts (live)

Mark Heard
Millennium Archives (CD)
Home Sweet Home HSHMH009 (2000)

Fourteen tracks—half are from the Fingerprint album; the rest consist of three demos of unreleased songs ("Morning Is Gold," "Night to Night," and "Tell Me It's Your Love") from Mark's days at Home Sweet Home Records, circa *Stop the Dominoes;* three previously unreleased instrumental renditions of Christmas songs; and a Gerry Howser interview with Mark about his 1985 release *Mosaics* (including audio excerpts from that album). "Remarks to Mr. McLuhan" is mistakenly listed as "Can You Hear Me."

Songs:

Epistle/Nowadays/Can You Hear Me/All the Sleepless Dreamers/Morning Is Gold/It Came upon a Midnight Clear/Joy to the World/O Come All Ye Faithful/Night to Night/Tell Me It's Your Love/One More Time/Just the Same/Es Tot [sic] Mir Leid/Interview with Gerry Howser

Various Artists
14 Number One Christian Hits (CD)
BCI Music BCCD1106 (2000)

This compilation of songs by Home Sweet Home artists contains Mark's "Heart of Hearts" from *Victims of the Age*. While that is one of Mark's more popular songs, whether it was ever a "number one christian hit" is at best a doubtful proposition.

Various Artists
Christian Rock Classics (CD)
BCI Music BCCD1108 (2000)

Mark's "Victims of the Age" appears on this compilation of songs by Home Sweet Home artists. The term "christian rock classic" might have been a little easier for Mark to swallow than "number one christian hit"—then again, perhaps not.

Various Artists
Trust His Plan (CD)
Time-Life 7243523468-4-4 (2000)

Contains Mark's "Castaway."

2001

Mark Heard
The Last Performance (CD)
Fingerprint Records FP0101 (2001)
A live recording of Mark's final concert (minus the song "Freight Train to No-where"), July 4, 1992, at the Cornerstone Festival. Released on CD-R by Finger-print as a fundraiser to benefit the Heard Family Fund. Executive producer: Dan Russell.
Songs:
Moment of Silence/Rise from the Ruins/Dry Bones Dance/Nod Over Coffee/ House of Broken Dreams/Satellite Sky/Tip of My Tongue/Orphans of God/ Washed to the Sea/Big Wheels Roll/I'm Looking Through You/Look Over Your Shoulder/My Redeemer Lives

Various Artists
CCM Legends: Christian Contemporary Music (CD)
Fresh Mix/Word CD33313 (2001)
Contains Mark's "Victims of the Age."

Kate Miner
(These Could've Been My) Greatest Hits (CD)
Cadillac Fund Productions CFP0875301 (2001)
Kate was a longtime friend of Mark's, and sang background vocals on several of his albums (she was then known as Pam Dwinell, or Pam Dwinell Miner after marrying bassist/producer David Miner). Three of these tracks were recorded in 1988 for *To Be True*, an unreleased project on Word Records, and several ap-pear on Pam Dwinell Miner, a 1994 promotional cassette. Mark engineered four tracks, mixed four tracks, contributed harmony vocals on "I Could Tell a Story" and "Under the Sun," and played mandolin on "If It's True." Kate also sings Mark's "Look Over Your Shoulder" with Randy Stonehill.

2002

Various Artists
Christian Music's #1 Songs (double CD)
Madacy Christian MC2 7241 (2002)
Contains Mark's "Heart of Hearts."

Various Artists
Paste Magazine Sampler, Issue 2 (CD)
Paste Media Group, LLC (no number) (2002)
Released in conjunction with Issue No. 2 of Paste magazine. Includes Mark's

"Nod Over Coffee."

2003
Mark Heard
Hammers & Nails (CD)
Paste/Fingerprint Records PM08 (2003)
Nine previously unreleased songs, two demos, and six bonus tracks from the albums *High Noon, Mystery Mind,* and *Adventures in the Land of Big Beats and Happy Feets.*

Songs:
Season of Words/Shaking/I Hang My Head/I Might Have Felt That Way/Hold Me Closer/I Always Do/When His Luck Runs Out/Backstreets/Your World or Mine/ Everything Is Alright (demo)/She Don't Have a Clue (demo)/We Have Let Freedom Ring*/Mystery Mind*/No*/Shaky Situation*/What Kind of Friend*/Jericho*

Liner Notes:
The previously unreleased songs on this CD were written during a three-year period from 1987 to 1989; most were penned in 1989. It was difficult period in Mark Heard's life. By the end of 1985, with the release his albums *Mosaics* and *Ashes and Light* (recorded in that order but released in the opposite order) Mark had finally escaped what had become an unpleasant contract situation with Home Sweet Home records. For a brief period, Mark and several other noteworthy songwriting friends (including both Tonio K. and T Bone Burnett) pursued the possibility of starting their own label together, advertising it through their personal mailing lists, and releasing a collaborative project. They had many living room discussions and even co-wrote a song together. The project never materialized, but mutating from those discussions came the formation of What? records. In 1987, the newly formed WHAT? label released Mark's album *Tribal Opera* under the band name iDEoLa. The album had joint distribution from both A&M and Word records, but despite the promising start of the label (which also released a pair of albums from Tonio K.) the label went defunct.

Mark was suddenly without a contract, and it would be three years before he recorded another studio album. However he still had several more songs written during that iDEoLA period, some of which he had made demo mixes of in 1987. He also continued to write new songs, and to shop them around. Demos of several of these songs found their way around, and some ended up on a pair of cassettes in the hands of David Miner. David was a successful producer at the time, and also both a friend of Mark's and an admirer of his music. Though no record deal ever came of the connection, David hung on to the songs. A written form of the lyrics also survived for all of the songs except for "I Might Have Felt That Way," and made their way to me shortly after Mark's death (along with the lyrics to more than 20 other unrecorded songs.) Finally, in 1990, Mark formed a new label, Fingerprint Records, with the help of friends Dan Russell and Chuck Long, and between 1990 and his untimely death in 1992 he recorded a brilliant trio of albums: *Dry Bones Dance, Second Hand,* and *Satellite Sky.* This album now become the lost fourth album of that series.

The opening two cuts, "Season of Words" and "Shaking" both were written in 1989, along with "Hold Me Closer," "When His Luck Runs Out," and "Backstreets." The songs lived on as simple demos recorded in Mark's home studio, primarily featuring Mark on acoustic guitar and bass. While "Season of Words" gives us a glimpse of Mark's introspective side, and "Backstreets" is an example of the social consciousness that marked all his albums, both "Shaking" and "When His Luck Runs Out" continue his tradition of real imaginary characters.

As may be evident from the drum machine and syntho-pop mix, "I Hang My Head" dates earlier, to 1987 and the end of iDEoLA era. The songs "I Always Do" and "Everything Is Alright" were written by Mark and recorded on Phil Keaggy's album "Sunday's Child." Mark added guitar work, backing vocals, some keyboards and additional engineering work to that album. When I first heard it, I instantly picked out Mark's songwriting (without looking at the credits) and remember thinking how interesting it was to hear Phil Keaggy singing a song that so obviously bore Mark's lyrical and melodic trademarks!

It was fun, years later, to finally hear Mark's own versions. "Your World or Mine" and "We Have Let Freedom Ring" also date back to 1987. The remaining written version for the latter of those begins the second verse with: "You can kill anything you want to kill—we know that war is hell /You can take any poison that will kill a member of your race." What he actually sings, however, is "You can kill anything you want to kill—we know that war is hell / You can break any heart you want to break as long as you break it well." While the sung version keeps the rhyme scheme, the written version has a tighter thematic unity dealing with the value of human life. "Mystery Mind," the only one of these to have been written in 1988, was previously available (along with "We Have Let Freedom Ring") only on a limited CD-R interview titled "Mystery Mind." "No," "Shaky Situation," and "What Kind of Friend" all appeared on the posthumous release High Noon. "Jericho" has perhaps the most interesting origin. Mark was hired to produce a collection of dance-beat remixes to a collection of songs, released by Myrrh on a rare compilation entitled *Adventures in the Land of Big Beats and Happy Feet.* He managed to get "Jericho" added to that mix. Whether he was embarrassed by the mix or not, he did it under the pseudonym Lee Cahuenga!

Matthew Dickerson
Vermont, April 2003

MARK HEARD COVERS

Artist	Song	OOG*	SHOL**	Other
Steve Archer	Eye of the Storm			*Through His Eyes of Love* (Home Sweet Home, 1983)
Carolyn Arends	Love Is So Blind	✓		
John Austin	The Big Wheels Roll	✓		
	Go Ask the Dead Man			*Authorized Unauthorized Bootleg* (Twitch, 1994)
Michael Been (of The Call)	We Know Too Much	✓	✓	*The Best of The Call* (Warner Resound, 1997).
Bob Bennett	Heart of Hearts			*The View from Here* (Signpost Music, 2002)
Big Faith	All She Wanted Was Love	✓		
bob	Fire	✓		
Bruce Carroll	Castaway		✓	
Chagall Guevara	Treasure of the Broken Land	✓	✓	
The Choir	Tip of My Tongue	✓	✓	
Ashley Cleveland	It's Not Your Fault	✓	✓	
Bruce Cockburn	Strong Hand of Love	✓	✓	
Jim Cole	Castaway			*Leap of Faith* (K-Tel, 1996)
The Company	Rise from the Ruins			Various Artists: *Fast Folk—the 10th Anniversary: Live at the Bottom Line February 20, 21, 22, 1992* (Fast Folk Music Magazine, 1992)
Daniel Amos	Strong Hand of Love	✓		
Marvin Etzioni	Hammers and Nails	✓		
John Fischer	Some Folks' World			*Some Folks' World* (Silent Planet, 1999) Various Artists: *Aliens and Strangers* (Silent Planet, 1999)
Steve Flanigan	I Know What It's Like to Be Loved			*Steve Flanigan* (Word, 1993)
Harrod and Funck	Worry Too Much	✓		*Harrod and Funck* (Heated Brick, 1997)
Jason Gay	Look Over Your Shoulder			*A Place Called Hope* (independent, 2002)
hezze	Another Good Lie	✓		
Iain	Watching the Ship Go Down	✓		
Glenn Kaiser & Darrell Mansfield	Threw It Away	✓		*Slow Burn* (Grrr 1993)

Artist	Song	OOG*	SHOL**	Other
Phil Keaggy	I Always Do		✓	*Phil Keaggy and Sunday's Child* (Myrrh, 1988)
	Everything Is Alright	✓		*Phil Keaggy and Sunday's Child* (Myrrh, 1988)
Colin Linden	Dry Bones Dance	✓		
Buddy and Julie Miller	Orphans of God	✓	✓	
Julie Miller	Treasure of the Broken Land			*Orphans and Angels* (Myrrh, 1993)
Kate Miner (with Randy Stonehill)	Look Over Your Shoulder	✓	✓	*Pam Dwinell-Miner* (Cadillac Fund, 1994) *(These Could've Been My) Greatest Hits* (Cadillac Fund, 2001)
John Mulder	He Will Listen to You			*Live—On the Way* (Narroway, 1990)
Rich Mullins	How to Grow Up Big and Strong		✓	*A Liturgy a Legacy & a Ragamuffin Band* (Reunion, 1993)
Olivia Newton-John	Big and Strong	✓		*The Rumour* (MCA, 1988)
Nickel Creek	He Will Listen to You			*Here to There* (independent, 1997)
Parmin Sisters	Rise from the Ruins	✓		
Pierce Pettis	Nod Over Coffee	✓	✓	*Chase the Buffalo* (High Street, 1993) "Nod Over Coffee" CD single (High Street, 1993) *Various Artists: Big Times in a Small Town: Christine Lavin Presents the Vineyard Tapes* (Philo, 1993)***
	Satellite Sky			*Making Light of It* (Compass, 1996)
	Tip of My Tongue			*Everything Matters* (Compass, 1998)
	Rise from the Ruins			*State of Grace* (Compass, 2001)
Leslie (Sam) Phillips	Heart of Hearts			*Beyond Saturday Night* (Myrrh, 1983) "Heart of Hearts" 7-inch 45 RPM single (Myrrh, 1983) *Recollection* (Myrrh, 1987)
Tom Prasada-Rao	Tip of My Tongue	✓		
Dan Russell	I Just Wanna Get Warm	✓	✓	
Jim Schmidt	Eye of the Storm			*Somethin' Right* (Emerald, 1983)

Artist	Song	OOG*	SHOL**	Other
Ramona Silver	Remarks to Mr McLuhan	✓		*Ultrasound* (Fingerprint, 1998) *Various Artists: Demonstrations of Love* (Prism/ESA, 1997)
Kevin Smith (of DC Talk)	Lonely Moon	✓	✓	
Randy Stonehill	Strong Hand of Love			*Return to Paradise* (Myrrh, 1989)
Swinging Steaks	Long Way Down	✓		
Kate Taylor	Satellite Sky	✓	✓	
Pat Terry	Mercy of the Flame	✓		
Tonio K.	Another Day in Limbo	✓	✓	
Vigilantes of Love	Freight Train to Nowhere	✓	✓	
The Wayside	Another Good Lie			*Live at Cornerstone 2000* (M8, 2000)
The Williams Brothers	House of Broken Dreams	✓		
Brooks Williams	Rise from the Ruins	✓		
Mark Williams	Tip of My Tongue			*Journals of a Recovering Skeptic* (Awakening, 1997)
Victoria Williams	What Kind of Friend	✓	✓	

   *   OOG—Various Artists: Orphans of God, Fingerprint (1996)

  **   SHOL—Various Artists: Strong Hand of Love: A Tribute to Mark Heard, Fingerprint/ Epic/Myrrh (1994)

***   This is a live recording—it contains a different version of "Nod Over Coffee" than the one that appears on Chase the Buffalo and the two Mark Heard tribute discs.

SONGS ABOUT MARK HEARD

Writer	Song	Recorded by	Appears on
Bruce Cockburn	Closer to the Light	Bruce Cockburn	Dart to the Heart (Columbia, 1994) "Closer to the Light" cassette single (Myrrh, 1994) Various Artists: *Strong Hand of Love: the Radio Special* (Fingerprint, 1994)**
Julie Miller	All My Tears	Emmyluo Harris	*Wrecking Ball* (Elektra, 1995) *Spyboy* (Eminent, 2001)***
		Tony Loeffler	*In the Texas Heat* (Orchard, 2001) *Bootleg Live!* (Orchard, 2001)***

Writer	Song	Recorded by	Appears on
Julie Miller	All My Tears	Julie Miller	*Broken Things* (Hightone, 1999) Various Artists: *Songcatcher* (film soundtrack) (Vanguard, 2001)
		Jimmy Scott	*Heaven* (Warner Bros., 1996)
Pierce Pettis	Trying to Stand in a Fallen World	Pierce Pettis	*Chase the Buffalo* (High Street, 1993)
Tom Prasada-Rao	Till I'm Free	Tom Prasada-Rao	*The Way of the World* (Ahimsa Acoustics, 1994)
Randy Stonehill	Mark's Song	Randy Stonehill	Various Artists: *Demonstrations of Love* (Prism/ESA, 1997)
Brooks Williams	Won't You Meet Me?	Brooks Williams	*Inland Sailor* (Green Linnet, 1994)

  * Includes songs "inspired by" or dedicated to" Mark.
 ** This solo acoustic version differs from the one released on Dart to the Heart
*** Live recording.

{ENDNOTES}

[1] According to Janet Heard, Mark was in the hospital for six days after the first heart attack. At that point, after doing the stress test on him, the doctors thought that if he rested for a few days in town, he could make it home to Los Angeles. Mark would need further tests and then either angioplasty or bypass surgery, but he much preferred to have that done near home rather than in an unknown hospital in the middle of Illinois. So he was released from the hospital. He went to a mall briefly to get some items of clothing, and then returned to the motel across the street from the hospital.

At the motel, Mark got on the phone with his sister Susan, and was reading from a book that Kate and David Miner had sent him. Janet does not remember the title of the book, but Dan Russell recalls that it was something about Gilligan's Island. Whatever it was, Mark started laughing so hard as he read to his sister that he was soon gasping for breath. Within moments he was dead. The E.M.T.s tried to get his heart beating again but they couldn't. They put him in the ambulance, with his wife and daughter in the front, and went to the hospital. On route to the hospital, Janet heard the EMT call ahead and say that the patient was dead. In the emergency room, the doctor did something and got his heart beating again, but his brain had gone too long without oxygen. Mark was in a coma, and never responded to anything after that. The neurologist did numerous tests, but never gave any hope that Mark could recover. He died of an infection about five weeks later.

In hindsight, one of the doctors who agreed that Mark could wait until returning to L.A. to have treatment for his blockages told Janet he would never suggest that again. The doctors had done what Mark had refused to do through most of his life: they had simply said what the patient wanted to hear.

² Bruce Cockburn, from the song "Closer to the Light" written about Mark Heard and recorded on the <u>Dart to the Heart</u> album.

³ The event, a predecessor to what has become New Sound's annual Inside Out Soul Festival, was held that year on the campus of Gordon College in northeastern Massachusetts.

⁴ "In Memory of Mark Heard," <u>Image: A Journal of the Arts and Religion</u> 3 (1993) 125—126.

⁵ Here is the gist of what I wrote:

Mark Heard truly was a treasure in a broken land. As any who knew him personally or have listened to his music will attest, he stands not only as one of the most brilliant and profound songwriters of our time, but also as a man of great personal integrity. Randy Stonehill, a friend and fellow songwriter, wrote:

"Mark Heard was a rare and bright light in this world. He was brilliant, sensitive, funny and one of the finest poets I am sure I will ever meet. His songwriting makes the majority of other writers' work seem pedestrian in comparison."

As evidence of this genius, some of the best songwriters and most gifted performers of our time have recorded songs penned by Mark Heard. That group includes: Joan Baez, Michael Been, Ashley Cleveland, Bruce Cockburn, Glenn Kaiser, Phil Keaggy, Bill Mallonee, Julie Miller, Buddy Miller, Rich Mullins, Olivia Newton-John, Pierce Pettis, Sam Phillips, Kevin Smith, Randy Stonehill, Kate Taylor, Victoria Williams, Brooks Williams, and the Williams Brothers. And yet, as has been the case with many of history's most gifted men and women, in his lifetime Mark Heard never achieved the recognition or commercial success that his lyrical and musical abilities deserved.

John Mark Heard III was born in 1951 in Macon, Georgia, the son of John Mark Jr. and Jean Heard. By the age of 20 he had already recorded an album and been offered a recording contract with Columbia records. But he turned down the contract, preferring to maintain his artistic freedom and integrity rather than be bound by the restraints of commercialism. This decision would characterize him for many years to come.

In the early '70s, as part of his own search for Truth and understanding, Mark traveled to Switzerland where he met Francis Schaeffer, an influential thinker, philosopher and cultural historian. Mark spent several months living and studying at Schaeffer's L'Abri. It is difficult to measure quantitatively the impact of that time, but it was certainly substantial. In Mark's music we see a rare and profound understanding not only of Grace, but also of our modern culture and human nature.

In 1978 Mark released his first publicly available solo album, *On Turning to Dust*, a collection of songs written and recorded over the previous eight years. During the ensuing eight years, he would record an impressive eight more albums, many of which still stand out as classics. But in 1986, after the release of his album *Tribal Opera* with WHAT? Records—an album recorded under the band name iDEoLA, though Heard himself penned all of the songs and played all of the instruments—Mark disappeared from the music scene for four years, a period that seemed interminably long to his fans.

Tribal Opera, despite its critical success, did not do well commercially. Meanwhile the fledgling WHAT? Records, after just three releases—the other two by Tonio K.— went out of business leaving Mark without a label. Reflecting on this *aspect* of the recording industry (if not this specific event), Mark wrote in his journal:

"Every station manager must worry that if enough people call to complain about a song and nothing is done, Joe's tire store down the street might pull its advertising. You have to play it safe if your livelihood depends on not offending anyone to this extent. Obviously, this stifles the creative output of aspiring artists—this imperative to fit the mold. Those who refuse suffer financially—which is also the kiss of death in a capitalist society that knows the price of everything and the value of so little." [see "The Radio—April 1990" starting on p. 137]

And so, having grown too frustrated by the entire music scene with its flagrant commercialism, and having been burned one too many times by the industry itself, Mark gave up his recording career. Or so he claimed.

Yet he could not stop writing songs. And his songwriting kept getting better. Finally, at the insistence of some friends including Dan Russell of *NewSound* and longtime friend Chuck Long, Heard was lured back into the studio to record some of these new songs. The result was *Dry Bones Dance*, an album released in 1990 on Heard's own newly created Fingerprint label. Though the label had little budget for advertising, word somehow got out and the album sold nearly 20,000 copies. Mark went back to the studio to record his next Fingerprint album, *Second Hand*, released in 1991.

Satellite Sky, Mark's third and final release with his Fingerprint label—and perhaps the most brilliant album of an already superlative career—followed in 1992. His hope was to eventually cull the best songs from these three limited-release albums, along with three new songs he had already recorded, and to put them out as a single album with a major label: an album that would be available to a much larger audience. About the time that *Satellite Sky* was being released, however, Mark was performing at the Cornerstone Festival in Bushnell, Illinois, and suffered a mild heart attack on stage. Amazingly, he finished performing the song, and then walked off stage with co-performers Pierce Pettis and Pam Dwinell-Miner. He was brought to the hospital where the doctors who treated him found two blocked arteries that would require surgery.

A few days later, before he was able to have the problem corrected, Mark Heard suffered a second, more serious heart attack that left him in a coma.

As Mark himself had written just a couple years earlier:

> The mouths of the best poets
>
> Speak but a few words
>
> Then lay down
>
> Stone cold in forgotten fields
>
> Life goes on in this ant farm town
>
> Cold to the lifeblood underfoot
>
> All talk and no touch
>
> And I just wanna be real

Mark Heard never came out of his coma. He died a month later, leaving behind his wife Janet and a young daughter, Rebecca, and leaving those who had known him feeling stone cold themselves. But he also left behind a legacy of phenomenal music that has deeply touched the lives of many people.

Though Mark is gone, his music should continue to touch lives; to knock just a few of the scales from our eyes; to leave us all a little bit warmer and a little bit more real; and maybe to let us know, despite what our culture has told us, that we are not Orphans of God after all.

[6] Milo Carter, "The Curtain Rises on Ideola's Tribal Opera," <u>Newsound</u> <u>Magazine</u> 2:5 (1987):16

[7] Ibid.

[8] from <u>Strong Hand of Love: A Tribute to Mark Heard</u>, prod. by D. Russell, C. Montano, and Jack Clark, Min., Fingerprint Records, 1994, videocassette.

[9] Mark Heard, "Stuck in the Middle," <u>Stop the Dominoes</u>, Home Sweet Home Records, 1981.

[10] This became the album <u>Second Hand</u>.

[11] Interview, Jason Harrod.

[12] "Anhedonia" is defined as "an inability to feel pleasure," having the same root as hedonism which is a pursuit of nothing but pleasure. Thus "pious anhedonia" would be an inability to feel pleasure, which actually causes one to feel a sort of spiritual pride.

[13] See "On Tour, Jan. 1979."

[14] <u>Strong Hand of Love</u>, Ibid.

[15] From Mark Heard's personal journals, via Janet Heard.

[16] Interview, Pat Terry.

[17] At the time Francis Schaeffer's titles included: <u>The God Who Is There</u> (England: Inter-Varsity Fellowship, 1968), <u>Escape from Reason</u> (England: Intervarsity Fellowship, 1968), <u>He Is There and He Is Not Silent</u> (England: Intervarsity Fellowship, 1972), and <u>Back to Freedom and Dignity</u> (England: Intervarsity Fellowship, 1972).

[18] Mark Heard, "With Broken Wings," on <u>Mosaics</u>, Home Sweet Home

Records, 1985.

[19] Mark Heard, "All Is Not Lost," Ibid.

[20] Mark Heard, "Heart on the Line," <u>Mosaics</u>, Home Sweet Home/Myrrh, 1985.

[21] Mark Heard, "The Golden Age," <u>Mosaics</u>, Home Sweet Home/Myrrh, 1985.

[22] Mark Heard, "Miracle," <u>Mosaics</u>, Home Sweet Home/Myrrh, 1985.

[23] Mark Heard, "The Golden Age," <u>Mosaics</u>, Home Sweet Home/Myrrh, 1985.

[24] In <u>Beyond Freedom and Dignity</u>, (New York: Alfred A. Knopf, Inc. 1971) B.F. Skinner writes "What is being abolished is autonomous man—the inner man, the homunculus man, the possessing demon, the man defended by the literatures of freedom and dignity" [p.200]. This passage is quoted in Francis Schaeffer's <u>Back To Freedom and Dignity</u>.

[25] Mark Heard, "I Want You," <u>Mosaics</u>, Home Sweet Home/Myrrh, 1985.

[26] Mark Heard, "Miracle," <u>Mosaics</u>, Home Sweet Home/Myrrh, 1985.

[27] Mark Heard, "I Want You," <u>Mosaics</u>, Home Sweet Home/Myrrh, 1985.

[28] Mark Heard, "The Golden Age," <u>Mosaics</u>, Home Sweet Home/Myrrh, 1985.

[29] Interview, Pat Terry.

[30] Mark Heard, <u>Eye of the Storm</u> liner notes.

[31] Ibid.

[32] See Genesis 1.

[33] Scheduled to be released by Brazos Press in the fall of 2003, the title is <u>Following Gandalf: Epic Battles and Moral Choices in the Lord of the Rings</u>.

[34] J. R. R. Tolkien, <u>The Hobbit</u>, (Ballantine Books, New York, 1966)

[35] J. R. R. Tolkien, "On Fairy-Stories," from <u>Tree and Leaf</u>, (Houghton Mifflin, Boston, 1989) p.52.

[36] Mark Heard, <u>Appalachian Melody</u>, liner notes.

[37] Ibid.

[38] John Fischer, <u>Harvest Rock Syndicate</u>, vol.7, no.4, p.3, 1992.

[39] Frederick Buechner, <u>Now and Then: A Memoir of Vocation</u>, (Harper Collins New York, 1983, p.16.)

[40] Mark Heard, "Lost on Purpose," on <u>Satellite Sky</u>, Fingerprint Records, 1992.

[41] Mark Heard, "Hammers & Nails," on <u>Satellite Sky</u>, Fingerprint Records, 1992.

[42] Mark Heard, "Treasure of a Broken Land," on <u>Satellite Sky</u>, Fingerprint Records, 1992.

[43] Mark Heard, "Look Over Your Shoulder," on <u>Second Hand</u>, Fingerprint Records, 1991.

[44] Mark Heard, "Dry Bones Dance," on <u>Dry Bones Dance</u>, Fingerprint Records, 1990.

[45] Interview, Randy Stonehill.

[46] <u>Newsound</u> Magazine 2:5 (1987) p. 17.

[47] Interview, John Austin

[48] Ibid.

[49] Interview, Tom Howard

[50] Email discussions in the Orphans-Of-God chat group.

[51] C.S. Lewis, <u>Mere Christianity</u>, (Touchstone, New York, 1996) p.191.

[52] Derri Daughtery, <u>Harvest Rock Syndicate</u>, vol. 7 no. 4, p.3, 1992.

53 Interview, Randy Stonehill.

[54] Letter from Prisca Sandri, written in the summer of 2002, related by Janet Heard.

[55] from <u>Strong Hand of Love: A Tribute to Mark Heard</u>, produced by D. Russell, C. Montano, and Jack Clark, Min., Fingerprint Records, 1994, videocassette.

INTERVIEWS

Tim Alderson, interview by the author, Glendale, CA, January 2002.

John Austin, personal correspondence with the author, September-October, 2002.

Chris Christian, phone interview with the author, August, 2002.

John Flynn, interview with the author, Glendale, CA, January 2002.

Chris Hauser, personal correspondence with the author, March-April 2002.

Janet Heard, interview with the author, Glendale, CA, May 1998.

Janet Heard, interview with the author, Glendale, CA, January 2002.

Janet Heard, personal correspondence with the author, February-November 2002.

Jean Heard, interview with the author, January 1998.

Jean Heard, personal correspondence with the author, February-April 2002.

Susan Heard, personal correspondence with the author, November 2002.

Steve Hindalong, interview with the author, Nashville, TN, November 200l.

Tom Howard, interview with the author, Nashville, TN, November 2001.

Steve Krikorian (Tonio K.), interview with the author, Hollywood, CA, January 2002.

Phil Madeira, personal correspondence with the author, March 2002.

Bill Mallonee, personal correspondence with the author, March 2002.

Buddy Miller, interview with the author, Nashville, TN, November 200l.

David Miner, interview with the author, Bristol, VT, January 1998.

David Miner, personal correspondence with the author, March 2002.

Kate Miner, interview with the author, Bristol, VT, January 1998.

Pierce Pettis, personal correspondence with the author, March 2002.

Joel Russell, interview with the author, Glendale, CA, January 2002.

Randy Stonehill, interview with the author, Seal Beach, CA, January 2002.

Tom Willett, personal correspondence with the author, November 2002.

Jason Harrod, personal correspondence with the author, September 2002 and October-November 2002

Pat Terry, interview with the author, Asheville, NC, October 2002 and personal correspondence with the author October-December 2002.

Chuck Long, interview by author, Asheville, NC, October 2002.

OTHER SOURCES

Carter, Milo (interviewer), "The Curtain Rises on Ideola's Tribal Opera," <u>NewSound</u> Magazine 2:5 (1987) pp.15++.

Dickerson, Matthew, "In Memory of Mark Heard," <u>Image: A Journal of the Arts and Religion</u> 3 (1993) 125—126.

Fischer, John, "Consider This: All the Shallow People," <u>Contemporary Christian Music</u>, June 1997, p.78.

Fischer, John, "Consider This: Heard Again," <u>Contemporary Christian Music</u>, September 1997, p.78.

Heard, Mark, "Life in the Industry," <u>Image: A Journal of the Arts and Religion</u> 2 (1992), reprinted in this volume.

"<u>Strong Hand of Love: A Tribute to Mark Heard</u>" (video), produced by D. Russell, C. Montano, and J. Clark for Fingerprint Records, 1994.

Porter, Tim "Mark Heard: Remembering America's Best Songwriter,'" <u>Paste</u> Magazine, 1:2 (2002) pp. 96—99.

{ABOUT THE AUTHOR}

Matthew Dickerson was born in Boston, Massachusetts in 1963 and grew up in the small town of Bolton about an hour west of the city. He had two older brothers, and later three foster Vietnamese siblings (an older sister and two younger brothers). His mother taught elementary school for a little over two decades, while his father spent two decades working with Logos Bookstores, first as a manager of the store in Harvard Square and then as Executive Director of the Association of Logos Bookstores. In his elementary and junior high school years, Matthew spent many days working at his father's bookstore. His "pay" at the end of the day was most often a book or record of his choice, which helped him to fall in love with music and reading at an early age.

After high school, Matthew went on to Dartmouth College in New Hampshire where he graduated in 1985, and then to Cornell University in upstate New York where he received a Ph.D. in 1989, before moving to Vermont in the summer of 1989 to start teaching at Middlebury College. His first novel, *The Finnsburg Encounter*, was published by Crossway Books in 1991. A few years later he became a bassist for the blues band Deep Freyed, for whom he also shares song-writing responsibilities with lead guitarist/vocalist/harmonica-player Bill Frey and drummer/saxophonist Daniel Scharstein. (On occasion, the band even lets Dickerson sing, and add some extra harmonica or mandolin to the mix.) With Deep Freyed, Dickerson has two independently released CDs, *Blues Oil* and *Faces of Blue*, both of which have garnered (limited) national airplay for the singles "A Fool and His Tongue" and "Statue Man" (both co-written by Dickerson). Along with this book, Matthew Dickerson also has a book on *The Lord of the Rings* (tentatively titled *Following Gandalf: Epic Battles and Moral Choices in* the Lord of the Rings) scheduled for release with Brazos Press in the fall of 2003. And he has a regular fly-fishing and outdoors column in the local paper, *The Addison Independent.*

He was introduced to Mark Heard's music in March of 1980 when Mark gave a concert at a small coffee-shop type venue in Bolton—the same night that the three foster Vietnamese siblings came to live with the Dickersons. However his personal acquaintance with Mark and Janet Heard didn't begin until 1985/1986. He remained in touch with Mark until Mark's death in 1992, and continues a friendship with Janet.

Currently Matthew Dickerson teaches at Middlebury College in Vermont and lives in nearby Bristol where he and his wife are at work raising their three boys on a 62-acre woodlot. Though his primary teaching responsibilities lay in the area of computer science, he has also taught frequent courses on the writings of J. R. R. Tolkien and C. S. Lewis. In 2002, he was also named the Director of the New England Young Writers Conference—a conference at which he had taught writing several times over the previous decade.